T0368135

9 ROUNDS
FIGHTING FEAR WITH FAITH

JULIE WHITLEY

WESTBOW
PRESS®
A DIVISION OF THOMAS NELSON
& ZONDERVAN

WestBow Press books may be ordered through booksellers or by contacting:

WestBow Press
A Division of Thomas Nelson & Zondervan
1663 Liberty Drive
Bloomington, IN 47403
www.westbowpress.com
844-714-3454

ISBN: 979-8-3850-3676-9 (sc)
ISBN: 979-8-3850-3678-3 (hc)
ISBN: 979-8-3850-3677-6 (e)

Library of Congress Control Number: 2024922097

Print information available on the last page.

WestBow Press rev. date: 11/08/2024

This book is dedicated to:

To you warriors. If you have ever felt alone, defeated,
or consumed by life's challenges, surrounded by
doubters who say you'll never make it, defy the odds,
overcome the obstacles, and keep conquering.

You're not alone.

With love,
JW

Contents

Intro

Fight

"Your Spirit is the true shield."
– Morihei Ueshiba

Adrenaline coursing through their veins, the anticipation rises. Laughter and banter flood the home. Energy surges through the air, competition brews between spectators, and the smell of hot wings, pizza, and sweat saturates the once-cozy living room. Nothing is more addicting than combat fighting; I enjoy every minute of it.

Watching a fight is much different than being a fighter.

With drinks in hand, we scream from the edge of our seats, cheering on our fighter. We bob and weave with them, attempting to escape their fate. The room erupts with shouts and cheers when a fighter takes a devastating blow. We scream, "Block, *duck*, GET UP!" The whistle blows, and the ref issues a warning.

We yell as we jump to our feet, "Are you kidding me? That's a bogus call." Our faces flush red with anger. "Is the ref blind? This is unreal." We slam our hands on the couches and shake our heads as they fall victim to blow after blow.

But imagine being the fighter. Training for months and weeks for a fight. Cutting weight, eating clean, training hard, and putting everything into mastering skills. Yet one thought persists. Was it enough?

The day finally comes to face the competitor. Although we prepared and trained hard for this day, something in us knows our opponent has been doing the same to defeat us.

"Keep your head in the game!" Walking to the cage, rink, or

mat, the sounds fade away until we stand face-to-face with our opponent and our thoughts.

Imagine that feeling. To be in a room full of thousands of people but feel alone in our thoughts. What does it feel like to push so hard and have our limits shattered time and time again? Proud of our accomplishments yet afraid it's not enough. Imagine being asked to throw a fight knowing that one's skill surpasses the opponent's?

This tends to happen in different seasons of our lives. In some seasons, we diligently walk with God (training hard). We remain closer than ever to Him, hearing His voice, receiving clear direction, and walking in power and favor. In other seasons, we lazily allow distractions to come between us and our "training" (walk with God). As a result, we tend to be less confident about our victory direction and even question God's presence.

Deuteronomy 20:4 (NIV) states, "For the Lord your God is the one who goes with you to fight for you against your enemies to give you victory."

Our coach, our Father, fights for His believers. He stays present with us in times of trouble and fights against our enemies so we can have victory. He dismantles obstacles that hinder us from Him and His purpose. All we must do is trust our coach.

This book was written for those with the Spirit of a fighter. It is filled with real experiences and pain. The kind churches often don't talk about (depression, anxiety, and doubt). Over the next thirty-six days, you will find that you are not alone in these feelings. Scripture is filled with Christ's followers, who struggled the same way—the fight is real.

There are many reasons why fighters fight. But after hearing many interviews and knowing a few fighters, the most common answer seems to be raw competition. A switch flips when we are put in a cage or ring against someone who has been studying us and training to beat us. There is no place for doubt or fear. We must trust our team and training and fight if we expect to be champions.

Our walk with God is the same. We have an enemy who studies us, knows our weaknesses, and exploits them in order to win the battle for our soul. We do not have time to doubt or cave to fear. It's time to harness the Spirit of a fighter and trust that God is in our corner. He has the vantage point and will lead us to victory.

It's my hope that as you read this devotion each day, you discover where God is in the midst of our darkest moments. I pray that each reflection and prayer brings fresh revelation and guides you on a journey of strength and healing.

ROUND 1

Taxed

Why Fight?

"Every thought is a battle, every breath is a war,
and I don't think I am winning anymore."
— Unknown

The whispers stir inside my mind,
Mocking me as I try to find
A glimpse of the joy that I once had.
The whispers roar that I've gone mad.

They say a slave I'll surely be,
To the pain inside of me.
Fear I'm losing this endless fight,
The whispers louder through the night.

Plagued by voices in my mind,
Lord, I wish to someday find
The glimpse of joy that I once had
Before the whispers made me sad.

The whispers stir inside my mind,
Mocking me as I try to find
A simple way to not annoy
The God I beg to restore my joy.

"Hands on hips, smiles on lips. I don't care if you're not feeling it. Fake it till you make it!" barked my high school cheerleading coach as we ran out to the track.

Grinning ear to ear in unison, we chanted a perfect cheer. Pom poms flying, backflips landed, and the crowd went wild as the varsity athletes took to the field.

Our job was to excite our players and engage the crowd, keeping the energy high throughout the game; to do that, we needed to look the part. That meant being as bubbly and spirited as possible while maintaining big, flirty smiles.

The football players trained to fight pain and strategize during practice. So did us cheerleaders.

Just like the football players, we were expected to have mental resilience. This was the hardest part of cheering for me because, unlike my peers, I didn't grow up in a private school. My parents sent me out of desperation to fix my behavior. They had no intention of keeping me enrolled when they couldn't afford it. But I had no plans to leave my school. I began working full-time, trying to keep up my grades, cheer, and do my household responsibilities. I was tired, stressed, and always on edge. But the field was no place to show any of that.

No matter what happened in our personal lives—losing a job, cramming for big exams, or even experiencing a bad breakup—we had to look the part. No excuses.

We became professional fakers, and we were good at it.

No one knew our struggles. The excitement of the crowd was contagious, and laughter and happiness filled the bleachers, easing our silent pains for the remainder of the game. Everything was great until we went home and no longer had an audience to entertain. Then, we were left to face our monsters alone.

Our Christian walk can look the same. "Fake it till you make it."

We fall into the trap of pretending to be okay, so we "look the part," especially in ministry. We may walk around with shallow smiles, pretending everything is fine. A few hugs and laughs followed by amens and "See you next week."

We look like we have it all together, filled with joy, peace, and wisdom, until we are in the confines of our own homes.

Lost in our thoughts and struggles, the monsters inside us like to rear their ugly heads—monsters like sadness or misery that kill our drive and hope.

I asked myself why I felt so down. Why did I have no joy? Why was every day a fight? "Fake it till you make it" never worked. I smiled on the outside, but inside, I was dying. Of course, I was "saved"—I loved the Lord. But where was the evidence of joy?

Joy is that elated feeling when you get a promotion. The rush of emotions when you have been trying to conceive and finally see a positive pregnancy test. Or that rush of emotion a fighter gets when they win a difficult fight.

If the prospect of getting what we desire evokes joy, then it's safe to say our well-being, achievements, and success would too. On the other hand, unmet desires can steal joy, leaving us feeling a deep sense of loss.

For example, an anticipated promotion awarded to a coworker, the scale not moving when trying to lose weight, a fighter losing a fight they trained hard for, or the loss of a pet or loved one. Lastly, the great unknown.

In the world of combat fighting, the cage has been called "the great unknown." It is where anything goes, where we are left to face the opponent who has been training just as hard to beat us. We enter the ring, uncertain if our training and skill will be enough to win. But we cross that threshold anyway. If we win, we're elated, but if we lose, thoughts of where we failed, how we can improve, and whether it was good enough consume us and plague our minds.

Joy is more than an emotion. It's the product of where we put our sweat, blood, and tears—hope for the outcome we desire. With unmet expectations, our egos take a blow, and we question everything we know.

Were we enough? How could we fail? Why didn't we see that? How could we let that happen again?

David said, "You turned my wailing into dancing; you removed my sackcloth and clothed me with joy" (Psalm 30:11 NIV). King David knew the pain of wanting to quit and exhaustion from the fight. No matter how afraid, desperate, or burdened he was, it made no difference. He knew the secret to redeeming joy. He weaponized worship, and he chose to fight. Worship drew the Lord close to him, restoring his joy. He completely surrendered his heart to God in all situations, believing that God was good and His ways were right.

The psalmist says:

> *"How long, Lord? Will you forget me forever?*
> *How long will you hide your face from me?*
> *How long must I wrestle with my thoughts*
> *and day after day have sorrow in my heart?*
> *How long will my enemy triumph over me?...*
>
> *But I trust in your unfailing love;*
> *my heart rejoices in your Salvation.*
> *I will sing the Lord's praise,*
> *for he has been good to me."*
> *(Psalm 13:1-2, 5-6 NIV)*

There it is. David, exhausted in the middle of his sorrow, questions God. Then he shifts gears to say, "I trust in your unfailing love...I will sing praise, for he has been good to me." Not "I may sing when I feel like it," but "I will."

He took the position of humility and held his thoughts captive, submitting them to God.

David proclaimed God's goodness even when circumstances did not show it. He chose to believe in God's unfailing love because of his choice to worship and surrender every season. God always showed up, restoring Him and His joy.

Reflection: What has stolen your joy? Circumstances beyond your control? Or perhaps a failure that has broken you. Read Psalm 13 and reflect on David's words. It's time to take the posture of praise rather than allowing defeat to define you. Let God restore the joy you once had, but trust that He is good, especially when you can't see it.

Prayer: Heavenly Father, thank you for your unfailing love. Please help me seek you like David so that I may trust your love and goodness even with a broken heart and my joy stolen. I ask that you restore my broken heart and bring my dry bones back to life. Lord, fill me with your Spirit, love, and hope.

In Jesus' name, I pray. Amen.

Fight or Compete

"I'll fight for you, but I won't compete for you; there's a difference."
– Unknown

"You don't understand. I love him with all my heart. I will do anything for this to work," I told my friend at church when I considered reuniting with my son's father.

"But does he love you the same? It doesn't seem smart to entertain getting back together if you're not on the same page. Look at how far you have come, how much you have healed. I know you're lonely, but don't settle for something that's not forever. I wouldn't go back unless you have a ring on your finger and a date set. You're walking right into a trap and will be back where you started."

That was pretty solid advice from a friend. But I didn't listen. Shortly after, I left the ministry and the church and moved in with him. I justified it by saying, "People don't understand that I need to fight for my relationship. Why would God want my son to have a broken home? We will finally be a family."

Within a year, I fell into a deep depression, trying to be a "good wife" and anything else he wanted. Nothing I did was ever enough. I pressed his uniforms at night, brought dinner and homemade baked goods to him at work, kept house, and cared for our son, yet none of it mattered. He was quick to remind me of how fat I had gotten, how I was no longer attractive or fun. With each hateful blow, a piece of me broke. My mind raced with thoughts of how I could fix myself to meet his needs. This fight with "the unknown" was in my head, and I was no match for this opponent. I felt isolated and alone. I lost good friends when I chose to go back to a toxic relationship after they had warned me against it. Yet I still believed that, someday, he would love me enough to marry me. Eventually, he was done pretending to want me, or even our family, and I was tossed aside like yesterday's trash.

Words can't explain my shame and pain; it was all-consuming. Knowing I was unable to function, my parents took my son for a week, hoping it would give me time to regroup. But it didn't. For days, I stayed in bed crying, no food, unshowered. Not only was my heart shattered, but so was my Spirit. My friends were right; my mother was right. I had lost my apartment, job, friends, and ministry, and for what? To be cast aside like I was worthless.

How could a person claim to love someone and dispose of them at leisure? How could loving someone with your whole being not be good enough?

After three days of looking at empty apartment walls and crying, a family friend stopped by and invited himself into my room.

He stood at the doorway and said, "Girl, you're a mess! When are you going to stop feeling sorry for yourself and get up? God never left. You chose to walk away, and even though you left, He is standing right where you left Him. So, put on your big girl pants, get out of bed, and clean yourself up."

With that, he left.

His words cut through me like a sword, but I snapped out of it. He was right; I had made excuses for my mistakes, and only I could fix them. It was not an easy road, but I learned a lot about myself and God.

The human heart can be deceitful; if left unguarded, it can lead us to make poor choices. Choices that we know deep down are unacceptable.

Some cope with stress by drinking every night, saying, "It's only one drink. I'm not getting drunk or doing anything wrong." Yet, internally, they are unsettled, knowing that drinking will slowly pull them away from their purpose. How about quitting a job without another job lined up? Some have compromised their worth by reuniting with an ex after multiple breakups and red flags.

That one is common. We hunger to be loved by another person so intensely that we will do just about anything to keep a relationship alive, even if it means losing ourselves. Of course, not all people fall into that category. But most have faced the pain of a failed relationship at some point.

My biggest lesson was in humility and learning that I didn't fail in the relationship. I failed when I expected a man to heal wounds only God could heal in me. I failed when I mindlessly walked away from God, hoping for Him to unite a relationship that was not in His plans. I knew God loved me, so with a broken view of love, I expected Him to answer my prayers, making me a wife and saving my son from a broken home.

When everything blew up, God's way proved better than mine. Psalm 86:15 (NLT) states:

"But you, O Lord,
    are a God of compassion and mercy,
slow to get angry
    and filled with unfailing love and faithfulness."

Though I compromised and fell short, God's love remained the same. He waited patiently as I struggled to make this marriage dream work. When it didn't, and the pain of rejection hit me one last time, He sent a friend to remind me He was waiting.

God loves us enough to send someone in our darkness. He loves us enough to fight battles for us. However, He will never compete for our hearts, which we must give him freely and completely.

We will face the pain of rejection or depression. That's just life. But that's not the end. If we allow Him in, He is our comforter, guiding us through pains.

Reflection: Have you entirely surrendered your heart to God? Are you compromising in your weakness and vulnerability to justify behaviors? Or are you sitting in the darkness of your failures, wondering where God's love is? Psalm 86:15 tells us that God is a god of mercy, unfailing love, and faithfulness. Yes, even when we are not. Reflect on Psalm 86:15. Ask God to reveal the space in your heart competing with His will and love. Then, write down ways you can surrender those things at His feet.

Prayer: Father God, thank you for your mercy and unconditional love in this conditional world. Although you don't have to compete for my heart, you still care for its condition even when I don't deserve it. Thank you for your faithfulness in my life.

Today, I pray that you reveal the broken places in my heart that cause me to doubt your love and compromise. Lord, I pray you help me release those things and restore a clean heart so I may be sensitive to your voice as it leads me.

In Jesus' name, Amen

Cornerman

"You do not need to pay attention to those voices within you that create pain or make you feel less competent, smart, able."
— Sanaya Roman, *Living with Joy: Keys to Personal Power and Spiritual Transformation*

I am a boy mom, but most of my friends have one girl. They say I lucked out because I don't have to deal with "girl drama" (a.k.a. emotional rollercoasters and mood swings).

I am not sure I agree.

My boys don't have excessive mood swings about clothes that don't fit or having the right makeup or hairstyle. They don't fight over who took whose clothes without asking or other things girls fight about. However, they still have moments; they process internally, which can be dangerous if left unnoticed.

My husband Matt and I don't usually see emotional outbursts; we see inward battles.

Each of my boys overthinks, overanalyzes, and gets in their own way. The first signs things are off are radio silence and emotional distance. When I see one of the boys retreating into himself, I know something is bothering him. I usually ask what's bothering them and get the same "Nothing, I'm good" response. Marriage has taught me that gets no results, so I give them space, allowing them to come to me. But one particular evening, I had a bad feeling in the pit of my stomach. Something told me space was dangerous. After the usual "I'm good," my teenager walked to his room and slammed the door.

That pit in my stomach sank deeper. I ran down the stairs after him, yanked open the door, and said, "You're not good, and you're going to tell me why because I am not stupid." After a few moments of arguing, without warning, the geyser in my son erupted.

Ethan's voice trembled. "You don't understand. I need to get a three-point-eight for D-one colleges to look at me. I'm trying to secure a starting position on varsity. I'm struggling in chemistry and can't get it together. Dad is always on my case, yelling at me, and you take his side." Hot tears streamed down his face, his breathing was irregular, and his voice rose to match his blood pressure. "Then I come home to chores that are never done good enough and endless amounts of studying and homework. I am tired, and no matter what I do, I hear something could be better. I will never be enough for Dad, for you, for school, or football. So, Mom, how do I fix that? Can you tell me how? No! Because I CAN'T!"

That pit in my stomach was right. His massive meltdown broke my heart. "Feel all the emotions, but don't stay in that place. You don't have to be perfect. Just do your best. Keeping things bottled up and overanalyzing while aiming for perfection will do nothing but give you a breakdown. There is always a better way, and you do not have to find it alone."

That night, I realized that getting the boys out of their own heads was where the battle started. We become their coaches, cheerleaders, and cornermen, providing guidance and support and helping them pick up the pieces of their broken hearts as needed.

A cornerman is a boxing term for a person positioned at the rink corner during a fight. Their job is to care for their fighter by sponging off their face, cleaning up wounds, and providing water in between rounds. They also watch the fight, study the opponent's moves, and find their weaknesses. The cornerman then gives their fighter tactical advice while cleaning them up.

From his vantage point, the cornerman sees things the fighter doesn't notice while in the middle of the fight. He pep-talks the fighter when he notices expressions of fear or defeat. He reminds him of his training and to stay focused. Sometimes, he calls a fight to protect the fighter if he has reached his physical limit.

The cornerman stays with the fighter at every step, from

preparing for the fight to completion. He strengthens the fighter's mind and fuels his heart.

Life is our boxing ring. We take swing after swing of failures, depression, and fear. We attempt to dodge anxiety, and then inadequacy blindsides us.

False expectations can corrupt our minds with the disgust of an imperfect life. Yet, we wipe off our faces and jump in the rink again without a cornerman, hoping no one will notice our weaknesses.

Mental health can be a hot topic today, causing turmoil within us and the church body. Our minds become places of shame and doubt when dealing with internal struggles. Endless thoughts and questions race through our minds.

Do we medicate a condition, or does that mean we lack faith? What happens when we pray and pray, yet depression still consumes us? Is there a place for me in the church where I am not like everyone else?

Being Christian does not mean we won't struggle with dark thoughts or depression. It doesn't mean we won't have insecurities or even doubt God.

But we can only stand in the rink dodging blows from our enemy for so long before tiring and giving up. The stench of defeat takes over.

But it doesn't have to be this way. We don't need to fight alone. Just like a boxer has a cornerman, so do we; his name is Jesus.

He has been with us from the beginning and will be with us until the end if we let him. He took beating after beating, knowing our enemy's weaknesses and tactics. So, we return to the corner where he waits to clean us up and give us directions.

Why, then, is it so hard to trust God with our pain? Is it because we fear looking like we have no faith? Are we afraid of other believers' comments? "You should pray more, maybe fast and pray. You do not have enough faith. God did not intend for us to live defeated…"

Whatever the reason, we need to remember this: Depression

is real, anxiety is tangible, and mental illness is genuine. But our authentic God can and will walk us through this arena.

No one should stop taking medications if diagnosed with clinical depression or other mental conditions. That would not be wise. Trust in the medical professionals placed in your life to help you. However, make God the center of your treatment plan. Medication alone can't heal the mind.

The fight starts in our minds, and if left unchecked, our monsters can defeat us.

Romans 12:2 (NLT) states, "Don't copy the behavior and customs of this world, but let God transform you into a new person by changing the way you think. Then you will learn to know God's will for you, which is good and pleasing and perfect."

It will be hard to discover God's will for our lives if negative thoughts and destructive patterns take over our minds. Copying this world's behaviors has done nothing but cause more pain than it's worth.

I have never met a person who has said, "I am so glad I spent the last five years trying to find happiness in the bottom of a liquor bottle," or, "I am happy I found peace from loneliness in bed with someone new." I never met someone happy about their drug addiction, which once numbed the hurt in their life but now has evolved into a huge problem.

This world shows me we are quick to self-medicate, lack self-control, and will do anything for self-preservation. The common word there is self. There is no room for God; we have it under control. But do we, or are we drowning in self-doubt, self-hatred, and lack of self-worth?

Well, the good news is, if we hit that low, we can turn to Romans 12:2 (NLT). "But let God transform you into a new person by changing the way you think. Then you will learn to know God's will for you, which is good and pleasing and perfect."

If we change our thinking patterns, we must be willing to allow God to change us.

But He can't transform us if we don't allow Him to. He will not force Himself into our thoughts or life. We must invite him into that dark place and trust Him to change us from the inside out.

Remember, He is our cornerman and has the vantage point; He sees things we can't see. It's our job to trust Him and follow His voice so He can lead us to victory over the battles in our minds.

Reflection: What thoughts are flooding your mind and causing anxiety, depression, or hopelessness? Once you have that thought, hold it against Philippians 4:8 (AMP): "Finally, believers, whatever is true, whatever is honorable *and* worthy of respect, whatever is right *and* confirmed by God's Word, whatever is pure *and* wholesome, whatever is lovely *and* brings peace, whatever is admirable *and* of good repute; if there is any excellence, if there is anything worthy of praise, think *continually* on these things [center your mind on them, and implant them in your heart]."

According to scripture, is the thought you're holding on to true? Is it honorable or worthy of respect? Does it bring peace? If not, it's time to do what Romans 12:2 (NLT) says: "Let God transform you into a new person by changing the way you think." Remember, God has the vantage point. The choice is yours; you can either trust Him and allow Him to change your thinking patterns or stay stuck in the toxic cycle.

Renewing your mind is a daily battle. Just when you think you have it under control, you don't. Therefore, you must hold your thoughts captive and place them under the lens of truth. If you choose not to hold your thoughts to the Word of God, you choose to walk in defeat. Do not feed yourself lies instead of God's truth and expect victory.

Prayer: Heavenly Father, thank you for the promises of your Word. Sometimes, I can't see past the darkness and lies my mind believes true. When this happens, remind me of Philippians 4:8. Give me strength from within that lets me know you are in my corner. The mind is the breeding ground from which all battles are formed. I ask you to please flood my mind and heart with your peace. Quicken my Spirit when I am in danger of falling into the thinking patterns of today's culture. Please deliver me from the bondage of fear and depression so I may walk in peace.

In Jesus' name, Amen.

Fighting to Function

"Life has many ways of testing a person's will, either by having nothing happen at all or by having everything happen all at once."
– Paulo Coelho, *The Winner Stands Alone*

I remember watching the movie *Creed II*. Like every fight scene, I was rooting for Creed to win. But then it happened: Creed took a beating in the ring with his rival that could have left him dead. The scene was so powerful that I had tears in my eyes. I watched as the fighter tried to process loss, pain, shame, and disappointment all at once. It was not the loss that took me back or the healing of extensive wounds but the look in his eye and his tone with his wife when he finally left the hospital. It was the "I am fine" attitude, the "I can do it myself" as he could barely stand and peed out blood. His wife stared at him, helpless, and went to his mother for guidance, stating, "It's like nothing really matters right now, including me" (Tessa Thompson, Bianca, *Creed II*).

This scene shook me because I have been him.

This moment brought me back to the day I stepped down from full-time ministry. That was my day of defeat. The day I realized I had sacrificed my family on the altar of ministry. To some, it would be an easy transition. Quit your job, focus on family, and get counsel, but for me, a piece of me died. I walked through my house as a dutiful wife and mom with an empty heart. What was my purpose?

I could relate to Creed, overwhelmed by depression and fear yet pushing others away and concealing it behind the duties of life to prove my strength or value.

"Life won't stop for me. I need to keep going," and "Too many people depend on me. I can't let them down." Yet, at the end of the night, I would tell myself, "If I can just smile one more day, people won't know I am dying inside."

Have you been there? Where you are in utter defeat trying to heal from one wound, yet life keeps handing you pain, frustration, and failed expectations?

We continue the facade of being happy because, as people of faith, we should be. Or we don't want others to feel bad for us.

So, we push through the days, hiding behind the mask of an empty smile, hoping no one notices our pain.

Depression is a bona fide enemy of our minds. It's sometimes packaged as sadness or feeling a bit off, infiltrating our minds with profound hopelessness and numbness. This deceitful enemy exists to keep us in perpetual pain and failure.

Sometimes, depression is situational. Some believers call it a spiritual attack. Other times, genetics cause it (believe it or not, people of faith can struggle with chemical imbalances) or even a mixture of these causes. Either way, we don't have to allow the condition to take us out.

Before I go further, please know that medical professionals should diagnose some forms of depression, which may need medication. If meds become necessary to overcome depression, please take them. Don't be ashamed or feel you lack faith. Instead, use wisdom and the tools God provides in medicine to help you.

However, we must also take responsibility for fighting the good fight and aligning our thoughts with God's Word. If not, we will relentlessly try doing things our way, all the while wondering why we are stuck in sorrow and bitterness, asking where God is in our circumstances. Naomi exemplified this perfectly.

Naomi, her husband, and her children left Bethlehem during a famine and settled in Moab (a pagan territory—they worshipped other gods). Unfortunately, her husband died, her sons married Moabite women (who opposed the law since the Moabites worshipped false gods), and they died ten years after their father's death.

With nothing except memories of their failures, Naomi returned to her hometown after hearing there were food provisions. But when she returned, she was not the same person they remembered.

When the townswomen recognized Naomi, she stated, "'Don't call me Naomi. Call me Mara,' she answered, 'for the Almighty has made me very bitter. I went away full, but the LORD has brought me back empty. Why do you call me Naomi, since the LORD has opposed me, and the Almighty has afflicted me?'" (Ruth 1:20-21 CSB)

Naomi meant to be pleasant. However, after losing her loved ones, a part of her died. Burdened, wrecked, and emotionally empty, Naomi wanted them to know God had allowed this to happen to her. She could not see past the pain of her circumstances and, in her darkness, felt God had caused her suffering.

We are no different. Some of us handle our mistakes or misfortunes with the help of friends or family, while others hide behind an empty smile so they are not perceived as incapable of handling their problems. Meanwhile, we are dying inside.

We are not alone. Many people before us, biblical leaders, warriors, and women of faith, have struggled with deep depression. Isaiah 61:3 (NKJV) mentions the Spirit of heaviness.

> *"To console those who mourn in Zion,*
> *To give them beauty for ashes,*
> *The oil of joy for mourning,*
> *The garment of praise for the Spirit of heaviness."*

Yet scripture shows us repeatedly through stories that God was with His followers every step of the way. They paved the way by showing us how to combat these negative feelings or spiritual attacks. We are no different; we need a reminder sometimes.

In Deuteronomy, Joshua led the Israelites into the promised land after Moses's death. Moses knew all too well the pressures and pains of leadership. So, he reminded Joshua several times, "The

LORD is the one who will go before you. He will be with you; he will not leave you or abandon you. Do not be afraid or discouraged" (Deuteronomy 31:8 CSB).

It's human nature to get overwhelmed by life's circumstances, especially when the odds stack against us. We suddenly lose sight of the big picture and fall into seclusion, trying to fight a battle that is not ours to fight.

The Israelites were famous for this; they always forgot how God cared for them in the desert when things seemed impossible.

Moses, with great faith, always interceded for them, bringing every complaint and problem to the Lord, expecting God to deliver, and He did, even when Moses failed. God was there.

Moses gave Joshua great advice before he passed—God will go before you and never leave you, so don't be afraid or discouraged because, much like the Israelites, we will forget what God has done when our circumstances are bleak, quickly getting discouraged. That discouragement will become an overwhelming depression we can't escape if left unchecked.

That's why it's important to meditate on His Word and remember that God will go before us regardless of how things seem. He has already made a way, and He fights for us.

Let's not become Mara. Instead, let's take a stand like Joshua and believe God has paved the way in every circumstance. Let's be like Moses and run to the mountain, seeking God for all things with great expectation.

No, we won't be perfect, but God looks for faith, not perfection. He will do the rest if we trust in Him.

At times, the struggle is more profound than we can handle alone. Anyone in that place should contact a pastor or a pastoral staff member and share the situation with them. Allow them to be in your corner, praying and helping you through this difficult time. Remember, no one is alone; God is good, and this shall pass.

Reflection: Is the weight of the world on your shoulders? Do you feel alone, just going through the motions, even when family or loved ones surround you? Is your mask about to break, revealing your hidden vulnerability? Whether depression is spiritual, circumstantial, or chemical, it affects our lives.

You can overcome each feeling no matter how destitute you feel. Regardless of the treatment plan you choose to get through this time, remember that nothing can replace God's living, breathing, active Word. He is your counselor, healer, and protector even when you can't hear His voice or see Him in the circumstances. Make God the center of your treatment plan, and watch Him restore your happiness.

If you feel your prayers are falling on deaf ears and struggle to believe God is present, seek counsel from a pastor or the pastoral staff. Allow them to pray with you, alongside you, and guide you through this season of life.

Prayer: Heavenly Father, I thank you for always being present even when I am not. Thank you for your forgiveness and love.

Today, I ask you to soften my heart to your voice. Allow me to hear you through the noise plaguing my thoughts. Reveal to me the strongholds hindering me from breakthrough. I bind the Spirit of heaviness that has tried to isolate me and keep me from your presence. When attacks come, allow me to stand, and when I can't, I kneel in your presence and peace. Thank you for your protection, power, and unfailing love.

In Jesus' name, Amen.

ROUND 2

Fighting Loneliness

Fueled by Abandonment

"She left you! They all did! Abandoned you! Shamed you!"
— Victor Drago Creed II

Fueled by rage, fighter Victor Drago retaliated against his father while preparing for his big fight against Creed. His father wanted him to fight for his family and his mother and reclaim the respect his family name lost when his father lost to Rocky. However, Victor was not looking for redemption for his mother, he was out for blood for his father. The pain of abandonment made him a feared and dangerous fighter.

Although this was a movie, it holds elements of truth. Not everyone who fights starts because they love the competition. For some, it is rooted in something deeper. Some are fighting out of poverty, to get off the streets, control an unchecked temper, or prove their worth. But regardless of why they are in the rink, they all chose the fuel that drives them forward, and for some, it's abandonment.

My biological father walked out on me a second time when I was sixteen. We had been reunited the year before. Things seemed to be going well. I was happy my prayers had been answered and my father had wanted me after all.

One evening, I overheard a phone call between my mother and him. "Are you serious, shorty?" my mother asked in an irritated tone.

"What do you want me to say? I didn't sign up for this." Urgency laced his voice. I held my breath on the other landline across our home as I continued to listen.

"Charry," he continues, "I have a child and family. I don't need this. I didn't ask for it." Tears streamed down my face as memories of all the promises he made to me just minutes ago flooded my mind.

"So, she's not your child?" my mother barked. "You have no

obligation to your firstborn? You walk in and promise the world only to run again? Typical shorty fashion."

"Listen, I need to go, but I will sign my rights away so your husband can adopt her. I want nothing to do with the cost of another kid. Tell her I am sorry and I love her."

"Tell her yourself, coward." She slammed the phone on the cradle.

A throbbing I had never felt before filled my chest. My throat tightened, and despite my effort to control them, tears continued streaming down my face. I gently put the receiver down. That was the last time I heard from my biological father.

That call changed me. Shame and anger overwhelmed me. After that, I would never trust another man.

I confided in my best friend. She tried to encourage me. "Socho [her nickname for me], I am sorry he lied to you. You don't need him in your life anyway. You have Lee. He has never treated you that way and always loved you. Don't waste another tear on a man that does not deserve them."

Anger pulsed through my veins, and I wiped my face. "I'm not crying because he left. He's not worth a single tear. I'm crying because my mom was right about him, and I was naive enough to believe differently."

Whether a parent walked out on us as a child or we face the rejection of a spouse, friend, or lover, fear, lack of trust, and loneliness leave an irreparable ache in our soul.

We adopt coping skills that keep us from feeling the sting of rejection, but it doesn't just go away. The feelings need to be dealt with head-on. Some wounds are more profound than others, but the healing process remains the same.

Before healing can occur, we must acknowledge the broken area and take the necessary steps to recover. Steps like defining boundaries, going to counseling, taking medication (if needed), and allowing time to heal. There is no shame in that. Admitting we are hurting does not make us weak or unable to handle life. Not dealing with it only causes further damage, keeping us prisoners of our resentment, pain, and bitterness.

David was anything but weak. He was strong, driven, and intelligent, and yet he stated the following when he felt abandoned by God:

> *"How long, LORD? Will you forget me forever?*
> *How long will you hide your face from me?*
> *How long must I wrestle with my thoughts*
> *and day after day have sorrow in my heart?*
> *How long will my enemy triumph over me?"*
> *(Psalm 13:1-2 NIV)*

I don't wrestle with good thoughts. No, it's the bad ones that I fight with at night. The bad thoughts plague my heart with sorrow and doubt. In those moments, like David, I cry out. "God, how long must I feel the pain of inadequacy, rejection, and loneliness?"

I was a broken child full of pain and disappointment. I became an even more broken adult as I faced repeated rejection from men who "loved me."

So, how do we overcome this overwhelming feeling of fear, insecurity, pain, and sorrow?

We trust in the Lord, not in our circumstances. Circumstances change, feelings change, but God's truth stays consistent.

"Trust in the Lord with all your heart and lean not on your own understanding; in all your ways, submit to Him, and He will make your paths straight" (Proverbs 3:5-6 NIV).

Reflection: Are you struggling with feelings of past hurt, abandonment, and inadequacy? Does the pain crush you at night, and you wake up struggling to smile?

You are not alone. Many great leaders in the Bible struggled. Today, I encourage you to ask the Lord, "How long?" as David did, then release it to the Lord and choose to trust in Him.

Prayer: Lord, I'm thankful you are the same yesterday, today, and forever. Please meet me in my uncertainty. Give me fresh wind and peace in the pain that I feel. Reveal your next steps for me and help me to walk in your peace as I choose to trust in your character over my circumstance.

In Jesus' name, I pray. Amen.

Training in the Desert

*"This is all you have. This is not a dry run. This is your
life. If you want to fritter it away with your fears, then you
will fritter it away, but you won't get it back later."*
– Laura Schlessinger

From the rearview mirror, Rocky says, "Come on, get up, kid, get up…That's it" (Sylvester Stallone, Rocky, *Creed II*). A beaten, exhausted, broken Adonis Creed slowly pulls himself to his feet from the desert ground. With determination and resolve on his face, he continues running, fighting the physical and mental fatigue. That's when his training takes a dramatic turn.

He becomes unstoppable, embracing the pain and refusing to give in to the circumstances around him, regardless of what he faced.

Some people think he's out of his mind for training in the desert, but I think it's brilliant. Training for a fight is hard enough; we must have ungodly self-discipline. But to put ourselves in a position where the elements work against us is different. We're no longer training in the familiarity of a gym. Instead, the conditions zap our energy stores faster than usual, pushing our dedication to a new level.

Something is to be said about someone willing to be broken, in body and Spirit, in hopes of gaining victory. It is knowing that the circumstance we face is only for a season. Even if the season is a bad one. Oftentimes, it's in extreme conditions that we figure out what we are made of.

I'll never forget the way I felt while waiting for test results in the doctor's office. For years, I had been in constant joint pain, swelling, numbness of limbs, and sleeplessness. Tests always showed I was fine, yet some days, the swelling and pain were so bad I could not get my shoes on. My normal CrossFit workouts got harder due to my legs and arms going numb or falling. I wanted answers, and this day, I finally got them (or at least some of them). "The test results show you have two autoimmune diseases, lupus and Sjogren's. Unfortunately, neither disease has a cure. But we can manage symptoms and make you more comfortable."

The words cut through the room like a knife aimed at my heart. That was the same disease that took my aunt's life and has slowly crippled a few others. My mind raced through the many women in my family who had passed or lost control of their muscles and were in constant pain. I went home with prednisone to lower inflammation and stop the joint pain. But the pain in my heart and mind remained untouched. The fear of dying the same death my aunt had plagued my thoughts and haunted my dreams. This disease had already started hindering my life.

"This can't be my story. This may be my desert, but I will not lay down and die here." I vowed to fight, and I never stopped.

How do we handle life's deserts? The dry places with no life, the broken and bruised areas. How do we manage failed relationships, marriage troubles, and addiction? How do we handle lust, pride, or anything else that sneaks its ugly head up, pulling us further into the desert and away from God's hand?

We have two choices: build resolve and persevere or stay on the ground, broken and defeated.

The choice was easy for me: persevere. Because staying broken is not an option. Having my children see me full of fear, a slave to my home and disease, is unthinkable. The thought of my sons lifting me from the couch, bathing, or changing me terrifies me. I refuse to stay broken, and I refuse to become a burden to my children because I gave up on myself.

I will fight for victory. No matter how hard it gets, I will keep fighting because, if I don't, the disease will win, and my family will lose. I will fight because God told me I would serve him in a great way. I will keep fighting for my family and hold that vision close, knowing that, one day, I will walk in that purpose. Nothing will take that from me.

To anyone lying on the ground broken and defeated like Creed, listen for the coach's voice. Dig deep inside and declare this scripture over life:

> *"Therefore, we may boldly say,*
> *The Lord is my helper;*
> *I will not be afraid.*
> *What can man do to me?"*
> *(Hebrews 13:6 CSB)*

No matter the obstacles knocking us down, sin can sneak in, making us feel unworthy. We must find the resolve to stand firm and believe the Lord is our helper. Don't bow to fear or defeat; grow from the pain and leave the desert stronger than before.

And we can if we listen to our coach's voice. God is our Rocky. When we are beaten down, He is looking in on us, saying, "Come on, kid, get up" (Sylvester Stallone, Rocky Balboa *Creed II*).

So, get up! Remember that dream the Lord placed in you. Remember a vision burdening you. Ask God to breathe life in those places again and listen. Allow God to help you by filling your heart with peace, hope, and strength when you have none left. If he did it for me, He can do it for you.

Reflection: What is your desert? Is it the bottom of an alcohol bottle? Is it the flirty banter with a potential interest? Is it a pain you relive caused by friends or family? What brokenness continuously leads you back to the desert? It's time to face and overcome it. Acknowledge the pain and the bruises it caused, and speak Hebrews 13:6 over your life. Don't allow anxiety and fear to keep you going back to where God is trying to remove you from.

Prayer: Heavenly Father, you gave me one life to live. Help me to live boldly for you with confidence and conviction. Help me train in the desert and grow from my pain but never remain there. Please grant me the strength to overcome adversity, the wisdom to not repeat my failures, and the peace that comes from walking with you.

In Jesus' name, I pray. Amen.

Reckless

"I feel the familiar pull—I am drawn, Icarus to his sun. I have been burned already, and yet here I am again."
— E.L. James, *Fifty Shades Darker*

There is a fire in his eye when he enters the ring. Moving in on his opponent, calculated and quick, they fall prey to hit after hit.

Jared "Big Baby" Anderson is swift on his feet, adaptable yet patient. Once he identifies his opponent's weakness, he strikes relentlessly and takes them down.

Some news articles have reported him as reckless. Fans have called him unstable, but the fire in his eye tells me he is driven by something more. And past interviews confirm that.

In an interview with Sky Sports, Jared Anderson states, "I'm just very irresponsible with my actions. I've just had some very reckless fights where I don't control my anger in the first two rounds and the opponents don't last."

There it is. That fire in his eye was the same fuel that drove me—fury.

Like a caged animal, I couldn't break out of the house fast enough. One girls' night, nothing felt better than tossing back a few drinks and decompressing with friends who saw me as something other than a maid and mom. I hated my life yet and felt like a prisoner. The only thing good in my life was my son, yet he was a constant reminder of the man I loved who did not love me.

After slamming back a few tequila shots, I was on the cusp of delusion. We left the bar, hit the package store, bought a big bottle of cheap Arbor Mist wine to share, and then staggered down the dark streets of an unsafe neighborhood. Once we polished the bottle, we parted ways, and I crawled up the apartment stairs to pass out.

Reckless, yes, but the anger fueled my impulses, and the consequences didn't matter. Nothing soothed my unchecked anger like booze warming my blood and numbing my mind.

Though these memories are distant, they seem like yesterday. Anger is the opponent that brings out my recklessness, and if left unchecked, I miss the voice of God (my coach).

A familiar pull of darkness calls. The innate, knee-jerk reaction to return to the broken places we came from, as if stepping into its toxic pool will magically heal us. Or maybe it's the seductive promise to heal the darkness hiding deep within that holds the magic.

"As a dog returns to its vomit, so fools repeat their folly" (Proverbs 26:11 NIV).

Warnings are disregarded while the thoughts plaguing our minds consume us.

Rejected by friends, family, and even church, why should we live in this constant battle the old yet familiar calls to us? Should we go or trust the unseen? Anxiety races through our bodies, our thoughts pounding like a relentless drum in our heads.

Where is He, this God we put our faith in? The one that loves, yet His people continually judge the likes of me. Why doesn't the church understand? Don't we serve the same God? Will I ever be good enough? Or will I always be seen as lacking faith, a person who does not pray enough?

Does God even exist? Or is He an absent landlord, leaving us alone in our vulnerability and weakness?

The anxiety keeps climbing, loneliness burns, and the hurt gnaws at our hearts, yet we stand before a silent and invisible God. We are in turmoil, a rejection of the "norm" and prisoners in our minds.

At least, that's what plays through our heads right before the slow fade begins.

Strategically, one compromise at a time, we give in to the reckless cravings. One drink becomes nightly drinks, one cigarette becomes a pack a day, a late-night text becomes a burning desire to feel his lips against your body. Each compromise leaves our flesh craving a little more. Knowing it's all wrong but, at that moment, it feels so right.

We will do anything to avoid feeling, to distract ourselves from this relentless cycle of irrational thoughts plaguing our minds until we realize the cost. We are left staring at two different people in the mirror. Recklessness cost me more than I wanted to pay. So, who is the woman in the mirror?

Pieces of her slowly die from each weakness. Numb, she dances with the devil in the moonlight and comes alive momentarily.

Yet, in the day's warmth, her eyes remain empty—a dim light flickering, longing for something more. The promise of truth, peace, and love. Was flirting with disaster worth the price? Will she ever be whole again? One woman, two choices. Who will you choose to be?

Anyone looking at two women in the mirror feels the battle between soul and flesh. Light and darkness cannot reside in the same space. They fight for souls, but each individual retains the final say, makes the final call. Will we hand the victory to darkness? Or will we suit up and combat the enemy, trusting that God will restore our brokenness as we submit to Him and His plan?

> *"Submit to God and be at peace with him;*
> *in this way prosperity will come to you.*
> *Accept instruction from his mouth*
> *and lay up his words in your heart.*
> *If you return to the Almighty, you will be restored."*
> *(Job 22:21-23a NIV)*

Putting our trust in the unseen activates our faith. First, we need to resolve that we know God's character. He is good, faithful, loving, and He is for us. If we fully believe in Him, we will rest in His peace, adhere to His instructions, and trust that His plan is better. It won't always be easy, but I have never heard of an easy fight. What would make the fight for your soul any different?

The choice is yours. Flirt with disaster and live an endless cycle of fear and pain. Or give up control, trust God's plan is better than yours, and watch as restoration occurs.

Reflection: Have you battled with loneliness, irrational fears, or anxiety? Have you been made to feel that you lack faith or strength or are just weak? These feelings can toy with your mind, leaving you in a bad headspace. If left unchecked, those feelings can lead you to compromise. Compromise starts with hurt, then isolation, and falls from grace shortly after.

If flirting with disaster seems more enticing than dangerous, it's time to get out of the danger zone. Reach out to a mentor, pastor, or pastoral staff member and ask them to help keep you accountable. Read Job 22:21-23a, and remember that submitting to God is an action, not a feeling. Feel his peace and presence in your obedience and grow stronger each day.

Prayer: Heavenly Father, forgive me for my weakness. Please give me the strength to combat the enemy's schemes. Please make me strong when my mind is weak and my heart is broken. As I hide your Word in my heart, help me hear your voice and know I am not alone. May you help me walk in peace and have victory in each circumstance.

In Jesus' name, I pray. Amen.

Diversion

*"When I get lonely these days, I think: So BE lonely, Liz.
Learn your way around loneliness. Make a map of it. Sit with
it, for once in your life. Welcome to the human experience.
But never again use another person's body or emotions as
a scratching post for your own unfulfilled yearnings."*
– Elizabeth Gilbert, *Eat, Pray, Love*

I feel like I am about to die. I am going out there to die, that's how I feel before I step out in the octogan," says Stephen "Wonderboy" Thompson in his YouTube video, "Fighters' Nerves."

I love that he created this segment to encourage and help fighters because it reminds them they are human, not superhuman. Every fighter will fight doubt at some point. They will face the invisible opponent of fear and anxiety. They stay in the back, calming their minds and listening to the voices of their cornermen, trainers, and support. When they step out to fight, we see a fighter full of strength and confidence, even in the midst of uncertainty. This is because they know who is in their corner, and regardless of the outcome, they will always be there.

I always pictured ministry to be a wonderful thing. A job where like-minded believers are driven by the same purpose and heart. I never pictured it being a lonely place where who you serve with would also wound you. Not long after transitioning to full-time ministry, my blinders lifted, and I realized that this job was (at times) worse than any secular job I'd held.

Surviving in this position requires thick skin and a soft heart because Christians and non-Christians need the same grace extended to them. I struggled with this balance because, although I had tough skin, my heart was just as tough. Every time I stepped into work, I felt like I was getting ready for a boxing match with believers. With every blow I received from a staff member or ministry head, my heart hardened. Resentment built and distance grew as each wound rooted deeper. I trusted very few and began to resent the place I felt called to. Yet I loved the people in the congregation too much to allow them to feel or see my struggle. Just like a fighter before the big fight, I stepped into church and wore my Sunday smile. The only difference was I forgot who was in my corner.

There is nothing worse than feeling alone in a room full of people, like a ghost among the living, haunted by the darkness of our thoughts—smiling and talking, trying to "keep face" from behind a mask and hoping the mask doesn't crack under the pressure of false truth. We try to keep busy by filling our time with things that make us happy to mask the pain and emptiness, hoping it will be enough. And for a moment, we enjoy the welcome distraction. It is how we protect our fragile hearts (or egos), preventing others from figuring out we are not okay.

"I'm fine. Things are great. I'm blessed," we say through a gritted smile.

But once life slows down, we are left alone in our surroundings and thoughts.

Inevitably, like a dark fog slowly hovering over a wet road, loneliness steadily consumes the space around us until we can no longer see what lies ahead.

We should be strong enough to handle this, smart enough to move on, and logical enough to know we are okay, but we're not. We should have enough faith to know that God is with us, but we can't see Him at the moment. Blaming our actions on faults, making ourselves the victims, or even God for the relentless ache that fills our souls.

We all must face an unwelcome enemy, the breeding ground for sorrow, depression, resentment, and envy. They are ugly emotions that, if not dealt with, create toxic thoughts that cloud our minds. Even believers can be crippled by loneliness. The craving for intimacy with another human has no bounds. Yet I find that we believers hide our pain to appear like we have it all together.

We have become masters of disguise, and to show great faith, we have formed empty friendships (as they don't know the real you), and the loneliness deepens. Toxic cycles become our norm. Put a smile on and perform for leadership to show we have great faith. We mask while we minister to congregants so they see how wonderful the Lord is as we encourage them in their walk. Encourage the broken and remind them of God's presence, but we remain hidden for what the mind knows our heart has forgotten.

Are we really showing them God's power by hiding our vulnerability? Or have we forgotten the feeling of His presence?

How do we break free from this masked pain?

Dare I say embrace it? Welcome the discomfort and process the pain. Invite God into that lonely place. He is waiting to be included in our brokenness. Though the heavy fog may surround us, sit in it, drink in the silence. No one is alone. Be vulnerable with God and patient while He ministers to our souls. Believe that no distraction or diversion can keep God from us. We just need to trust Him as he leads us through the sleepless nights and streams of tears.

We can't stay masked forever; there is no place to hide that God can't see us. So why not surrender our vulnerability and pain to him and allow God to show us what we are truly made of?

Psalm 139:7-10 (CSB) states:

> "Where can I go to escape your Spirit?
> Where can I flee from your presence?
> If I go up to heaven, you are there;
> if I make my bed in Sheol, you are there.
> If I fly on the wings of the dawn
> and settle down on the western horizon,
> even there your hand will lead me;
> your right hand will hold on to me."

David states there is nowhere he can hide that the Lord will not be. Isn't that encouraging? When David sat in the cave, afraid and alone, God brought him comfort and strength. No matter where David was, the Lord was with him. We have the same access to the Lord as David. However, we must seek Him out in our pain and believe He will be our comforter. We must be transparent and authentic regardless of what that may look like. If that means feeling the weight of loneliness, we must endure it, believing God will meet us in that pain. We need to reach for His hand and not the hands of others in hopes of soothing the pain.

No other person can fill the void or rekindle our happiness. So, it's time to stop running from what is broken in us, using ministry opportunities as a diversion, or we will stay broken.

As long as we try to fill that space with someone or something else, we leave no room for God to be our comfort or strength.

We must invite Him into our pain and allow Him to walk us through it. Only then can we see God move in our circumstances and bring us real peace.

Reflection: Are you guilty of recruiting friends or family to fill the loneliness void? Have you felt disappointed and hurt when those people could not distract you from that dark place? Read and reflect on Psalm 139:7-10 and tell yourself, "If David could not escape God's presence, neither can I." Recite the scripture using yourself instead of David and allow God to take his rightful place as captain and leader of your life. Allow Him to lead you out of your pain. Remember, He is with you.

Prayer: Heavenly Father, the fog of loneliness has clouded my vision. I need you to clear the path and bring me peace. Help me embrace the discomfort as I grow. Please forgive me for trusting the comfort of man over trusting your presence. Please be my comforter and strength.

In Jesus' name, we pray. Amen.

ROUND 3

Fighting Despair

Spirit of a Fighter

"I never thought of losing, but now that it's happened, the only thing is to do it right. That's my obligation to all the people who believe in me. We all have to take defeats in life."
— Muhammad Ali

Over the last year, my son Ethan has joined me at CrossFit. Picking me up from the gym and walking in on a few workouts motivated him to try the sport. He was the youngest athlete, but he didn't care. He showed up and did his best. But I was not the one who inspired him. Our coach's son earned that honor.

My son gravitated toward this incredible young man: a college student, hard worker, amateur MMA fighter, and CrossFitter. Every time we came to work out, he would scan the room to see if a box was open near Joe, and Ethan would push himself hard to keep up with him. Had we stayed members at the gym, I am sure he would have requested mentorship from Joe.

One evening, the coach announced that Joe's first fight was scheduled and tickets were on sale. Ethan watched Joe train hard and cut weight and listened when he spoke to others about his journey and upcoming fight. Unfortunately, we could not go on the night of Joe's big event, but the news was plastered on social media afterward. It was a close fight, and Joe gave it his all, but in the end, he lost. My son was devastated for him. However, when we saw Joe at the gym, his energy sang a different tune, like losing was no big deal. It motivated him to train better for the next fight—which he won with a KO in twenty-three seconds.

My son witnessed something great during this time. He learned what it looked like to have the Spirit of a fighter. He watched from the sidelines as a young man gave his all and lost. But he watched him get up, dust off, and keep moving forward with a positive and healthy attitude. Joe's perseverance and drive inspired Ethan more. Though Joe's attitude and actions paid off when he won his next fight, it goes deeper than that. He decided how he wanted to appear as a fighter and person. Joe maintained his head, Spirit, and character and moved forward with pride and confidence. The way he carries himself as a person off and on the mat speaks to my son and everyone who watches him.

How we respond when life knocks us down matters. When we are overwhelmed with disappointment, grief, or tiredness, do we give up? Do we become bitter and resentful? Do we stay in defeat or rise to the occasion and trust God to lessen the burden?

Scripture says,

> "Cast your burden on the LORD,
> and he will sustain you;
> he will never allow the righteous to be shaken."
> (Psalm 55:22 CSB)

Joe is an incredible young man, but that's because he has amazing parents guiding him. Our coach, his mother, helped carry his burdens in private. She spoke life to him so fear of failure would not shake him.

If a mother can help carry the burden in his time of trouble and disappointment, how much more would God?

Sometimes, we feel beaten down, crushed, or even defeated. But we don't have to stay there. We are children of God. We must walk out our faith, even in the ugly parts. Sometimes, walking it out means dusting ourselves off, releasing the pains to the Lord, and trusting that He will sustain us and equip us for what is ahead. It's time to have a fighter's Spirit and stop living in defeat.

Reflection: Were you just given the knockout blow and are down for the count? Are you grappling with the pain of defeat or grieving, wondering if the fight is worth it? The answer is yes. Remember, the Spirit of God lives inside you. He will fight for you. First, you need to do your part. Read Psalm 55:22 and reflect on what it means to cast your burdens upon the Lord. Then, list all the things hindering you from moving forward and lay them at His feet.

Prayer: Heavenly Father, thank you for always being present in my circumstances, even if I don't see you. Please show me how to release my burdens so I can walk in your peace. Thank you for sustaining me in my time of need and strengthening me when I am broken.

In Jesus' name, Amen.

Trust in Despair

"When nothing matters, then I thought there was no point in living. I do want to die, and I prayed for death on a daily basis," Tyson Fury said in an interview where he speaks out about mental health and depression. Fury is the former lineal heavyweight champion. He was unrivaled in the ring.

He had it all, family, money, and respect, yet he still found himself in a place of darkness. People wonder how a person who has it all wishes to throw their life away, but Tyson said it best. "When nothing matters..." A man who fights for a living and knows about physical and mental toughness could not fight his way out of this place, and I know the feeling.

In 2014, I found out I was pregnant. I dreamed not long before that I was holding a girl who looked just like me and gave her a name. However, within two months, that promise came to an end. Waves of emotions drowned me—anger, sadness, frustration, disappointment, and then the deepest depression. Nothing mattered to me. Why would God promise me something and then take it away? During this season, I also had my first speaking engagement and the district women's retreat. I didn't know how I was going to do it. How could I speak of a good God when He hurt me so badly? But I did. I preached a week after the loss of our baby. I cried and spoke of the pain but how God was meeting me in dark places. Healing is a process, it doesn't just happen, and if people say differently, they are lying to themselves and you.

Believers are not exempt from struggling with grief, anxiety, or feelings of hopelessness. I wish I could say they were, but that is far from the truth. When a person of faith mentions such pains, they can feel they lack faith or simply don't trust God.

All humans (even believers) struggle with these feelings at some point. Job, a man of God, says this:

> *"And now my life seeps away.*
> *Depression haunts my days.*
> *At night my bones are filled with pain,*
> *which gnaws at me relentlessly.*
> *With a strong hand, God grabs my shirt.*
> *He grips me by the collar of my coat.*
> *He has thrown me into the mud.*
> *I'm nothing more than dust and ashes.*
> *'I cry to you, O God, but you don't answer.*
> *I stand before you, but you don't even look.'"*
> *(Job 30:16-20 NLT)*

This is the very essence of pain and hopelessness. Job's significant loss merited his despair. He lost his children, wealth, home, provisions, health, and the trust of his friends. His wife tried to get him to curse God for all the tragedy and loss they experienced. Yet, despite all his pain, he stayed faithful to God.

This story reminds us that even God's children face impossible times; sometimes, it may be more than we can handle on our own. However, we can persevere in our circumstances. How?

Trust and understanding root our relationship with God. Job trusted and loved the Lord. Even when he was hurt and questioned God, he never turned away. He trusted in God's sovereignty, love, and who He was to him. That type of trust only comes from feeding our faith daily, strengthening our souls so we are grounded in truth when trials come (and they will).

We may not know what to do. We may cry to sleep, we may

pray to die, or even hear the voices of friends trying to help, yet feel worse. But if we trust God despite what's happening around us, we can be confident that He will guide us to brighter days.

Tyson Fury prayed for death, yet he is still alive. He is alive because the Lord has a purpose for him, and through his ashes, he was reborn, now helping other fighters fight the same monster that tried to take him out.

If God did it for him and me, won't he do it for you?

"Trust in the LORD with all your heart; do not depend on your own understanding. Seek his will in all you do, and he will show you which path to take" (Proverbs 3:5-6 NLT).

Reflection: Are you in a place where nothing matters? Where nothing seems to hold value to you? Depression is an opponent that has no bounds. There is no telling when it will pop up and how long it will stay. But you do not have to fight it alone. If you are in this space, know that you have a purpose. God has a plan for you, even if you don't see it or even if you don't care.

Print Proverbs 3:5-6 and place it where you can see it daily. Allow it to be a reminder and feed your soul. Then, reach out to a trusted pastor or mentor. Make your struggle known so they can help carry your burden. Allow them to pray with you and for you, walking you through this season when you don't have the strength to do it alone. If the depression goes past the realm of a pastoral team, there is no shame in seeking a professional. Find a good counselor to help you navigate what is happening in your mind so you too can overcome.

Prayer: Lord, please show yourself to me in this dark place. Please meet me where others can't. Give a word that will resonate deeper than the darkness. Please lift me from this place while I put what's left of my faith into trusting you.

In Jesus' name, I pray. Amen.

Choke Hold

"I am not in this world to live up to your expectations,
and you're not in this world to live up to mine."
— Bruce Lee

My parents raised us watching fight night. Whether it was boxing or UFC, if a fight was on, we were watching. At first, I didn't understand the fascination of watching someone become another person's punching bag. But one UFC match changed my mind. I watched a fighter fight like his life depended on it. Tears filled my eyes as I watched in disbelief; the man continued to get up even when he could barely stand. "Dad," I cried out. "This is terrible, barbaric. Why won't they stop the fight? Why won't he just stay down?"

My dad smiled and said, "Julie, watch. Look at his face. He still has fight left."

And sure enough, my dad was right. The battered fighter flipped the fight with a submission move called a choke hold. In one move, he cut the blood supply off to his opponent's head, leaving him helpless and tapping out in seconds. I couldn't believe it. I was shocked and excited at what I witnessed. But most importantly, I learned a lesson that shaped my thought pattern for the rest of my life. Never throw (quit) a fight. No matter how bad it gets, stand back up.

Drive is a psychological response birthed from deep within. It can be both a powerful tool and a dangerous one.

Jealousy can drive a person to murder. Depression can drive someone to suicide. Lust can drive us to sexual immorality, and greed can drive us to steal.

Sometimes, our drive to prove our worth to others leaves us trapped in an endless cycle of misery and pain.

Drive is "An aroused state of psychological tension that typically arises from a need. A drive, such as hunger or thirst, motivates the organism to act in ways that will reduce the tension. So, for example, when you become hungry (tension caused by need for food) you are motivated to eat (method of reducing the tension)."[1]

When tensions run high and we feel the pressure to execute something, whether in sport, a personal goal, or a job, we find an untapped resolve to get it done at all costs. This type of drive often shows up in the workplace or school. We add more to our plates to prove we can handle the load and do everything. But is that the life we want to live? Or are we setting unrealistic expectations for ourselves for others' approval?

For me, it was approval. Starting in high school, I turned the pain others placed on me into armor. Every time I heard, "Julie, you will never become a writer. You can't spell," or, "You're not smart enough to do or be…" I channeled my inner fighter and refused to allow the choke hold of their words to define me. I was relentless in my pursuit to prove them wrong. My drive grew and grew until it took over. Whatever I put my hands to, I wanted to be the best at and would work myself to exhaustion to see it happen.

There is nothing wrong with wanting to be great at something. But it should not stir up a hunger so deep we sacrifice our peace or joy. When focused on the pressure of expectation, our desire to please man, not God, drives us.

In Mark, right after Jesus's baptism, he was led by the Spirit into the wilderness. "At once the Spirit sent him out into the wilderness, and he was in the wilderness forty days, being tempted by Satan. He was with the wild animals, and angels attended him" (Mark 1:12-13 NIV).

Forty days and nights in the wilderness, tormented by the devil, he remained rooted in truth. The enemy had great expectations of

---

[1] AlleyDog.com, https://www.alleydog.com/glossary/definition. php?term=Drive.

him. He was asked to prove his power and deity. Yet he remained humble and steadfast to God's Word. We can learn a lot about Jesus's position in this passage—one of surrender, humility, and strength. He knew who he was and proved nothing. We can strive to walk in the same manner, not fighting to prove our worth.

First, when things stack against us, don't look for the quickest way to relieve the pressure. Submit to the process and ask God for wisdom.

Second, trust that God has us covered in our pain and will minister to us if we seek Him in our desperation (not our friends and family first).

Third, we should know who we are in Christ and not expect to acquire our value in man. This means consistently being in God's Word, strengthening us in Spirit and truth.

When we apply those steps in our life, our drive will be to please God, and our flesh will submit to the Spirit's leading. This may not be easy. We will face this battle daily, just as Jesus did for forty days. But it is possible, and when we realize that other people's expectations don't define us or hold a bearing on who we are, the pressure of expectations lifts off our shoulders.

Reflection: Are you struggling with the pressure of expectations? Are you in an endless cycle of proving your worth to man? Are you feeling overworked and undervalued? I have been there, it's an exhausting place. Know that you were not designed to prove your worth. You should not be living in constant turmoil and stress with no peace. Take the time to read Mark 1:12-13.

Put yourself in Jesus's shoes. Ask yourself if you are walking humbly. Are you trusting the Father or falling for the temptations of the enemy? Are you rooted in your word, getting fed daily? And do you know who you are?

Prayer: Heavenly Father, thank you for your Word. Today, I ask that you bring me clarity and wisdom and show me who I am. Please show me what I need to release to have peace. Show me how to walk in your peace and presence so that I can be free from the pressure of expectations.

In Jesus' name, we pray. Amen.

Hit the Mat

"Remember that stress doesn't come from what's going on in your life.
It comes from your thoughts about what's going on in your life."
– Andrew J. Bernstein

I t was a long day—the kind of day where nothing went right and nothing got done. The tension continued climbing as I replayed everything that went wrong and all my failed accomplishments before my kids walked through the door from school.

While attempting to shift gears to help with homework, cook dinner, and prep for the morning, my kitchen suddenly transformed into a fighting ring. I became the referee in the boys' battle of wills. Finally, I had enough. I shouted, "Get out of my kitchen now before I break all your legs!"

My husband responded, "Whoa, babe, take it easy. It's not that bad. You need to leave and get to the gym."

I shot him the look of death.

Though I was furious, I knew he was right. The gym had become my therapy in times of stress. If I couldn't be there, those closest to me paid the price of my explosions. Of course, I would feel bad afterward and try to make things right, but apologies were not enough. I needed to get ahold of my frustrations and handle stress better.

Stress is when physical, mental, or emotional tensions are so high they trigger mental responses like worry, frustration, anger, and even depression. So, how do we combat such a powerful response to life's challenges?

Not having control is scary. We want things done right the first time without flaws or complications. So, when something does not meet our expectations, we lose it a bit. First, we must acknowledge that we can't control what happens around us but can control our responses.

But scripture says, "Can any of you add one moment to his life span by worrying?" (Matthew 6:27 CSB).

Though we can't add moments or solve problems by worrying and stressing out, we tend to do it anyway. But of course, God already knew that. He gave us the scripture to remind us that He clothes the grass and cares for the birds. We just forget that we are the crown of His creation, and He will do the same, if not more, for us. We just need to release control and have faith. So, the next time things start going wrong, try changing your perspective. Focus on a different angle, and trust that God will work out the details.

Reflection: Finding peace in the middle of chaos is never easy. Trying to remain calm when things are falling apart around you is easier said than done, but it can be done. If you struggle with stress and trusting in uncertain times, read Matthew 6:25-30. Remember that moments can't be added to life by stressing over what has happened or will happen. The only thing we can do is trust the Lord will provide for us as he did the birds of the sky and the grass of the fields.

Prayer: Heavenly Father, thank you for your Word. Thank you for providing for all my needs, those you have met and will meet. Please bring me peace while I strengthen my faith through my trials. Please reveal yourself in my circumstances and grant me peace.

In Jesus' name, I pray. Amen.

ROUND 4
Submission

Break the Pattern

"You're not stuck. You're just committed to certain patterns of behavior because they helped you in the past. Now, those behaviors have become more harmful than helpful. The reason why you can't move forward is because you keep applying an old formula to a new level in your life. Change the formula to get a different result."
– Emily Maroutian

Hit the gym, eat healthy, watch some tape, repeat. Hours of time go into training for a fight. These athletes spend most of their days in active physical training under their team's direction. When they are not in physical training, they are watching tape of their opponents' previous fights. The fighter and trainers watch carefully to identify patterns and weaknesses opponents show in an effort to gain a vantage point.

Seeing your opponent's weakness is not good enough; you then need to be willing to make those areas your strength. If a fighter is not adaptable and unwilling to grow, they will stay stuck, and their career will be short-lived. A fighter needs to do whatever it takes to win. This includes staying teachable and adaptable, willing to embrace change.

This was one of the hardest things for me to do during my career change three years ago—from owning my own business as a daycare provider to becoming a personal trainer. My vision was to help women and inspire them to be the best form of themselves physically, mentally, and spiritually. But this vision came at a price, and, at times, I questioned whether it was worth it.

Looking at our lives like we are watching tape can be easy. We can get discouraged by where we are or what we see. Yet, we have a vision that is just out of grasp. Working hard day and night to achieve our goals, we make little progress no matter how hard we try. Our work has been in vain because we continue running in circles and getting nowhere. Defeated, the weight of failure and frustration presses down, and we feel stuck.

To be productive, we must move past "stuck" and grow from that place. Colossians 3:2 (CSB) states, "Set your minds on things above, not on earthly things."

Our patterns of thinking develop through our life experiences. Some of these patterns are used for survival, protection, and promotion. However, when we give our lives to God, He makes us new. Therefore, our way of thinking should reflect that. The problem lies in using our old mindset to accomplish our new goals, but that will no longer work; we are a new creation.

If we want success, we need to trust God in all areas. First, listen to the directions we should take with our families, work lives, and marriages. Then, trust that God's way is better than ours and apply it instead of trying to open our own doors. A kingdom mindset makes no worldly sense, yet God's way is perfect. Change your mindset and change your outcome.

Reflection: What areas in life feel stagnant? Have you filtered those thoughts through God's Word and will? Reflect on Colossians 3:2 and remember that as you stay focused on things above, they may not always align with earthly logic. Rest assured, God has clear plans for you. If you shift your mindset to trust God's way, you will witness progress in all areas of your life.

Prayer: Heavenly Father, thank you for your vision, drive, and motivation. Thank you for giving me the desire to be better in all areas of life. But as the demands of change surround me, I pray you help me stay focused on you and the promises in your Word. Please bring peace in times of doubt and understanding when fear threatens my thoughts.

In Jesus' name, I pray. Amen.

Trust the Process

"We usually focus on what we're doing or where we're going, but God's primary concern is who we're becoming in the process."
— Mark Batterson, *The Circle Maker*

During the pandemic, I was burned out from watching children and felt my children got the worst of me. My husband and I discussed my career change. It was time to close the doors to the daycare and do something else. "Why don't you become a CrossFit coach or trainer and make that your ministry," my husband said.

I laughed. Doubt instantly filled my mind, and the questions poured in. What could I possibly offer women? I don't look as fit as most trainers. Was I good enough?

After listening to the doubt replay in my head, I laughed off the idea and said, "Do you know how expensive it is? And the risk?"

As if he knew what I would say, Matt replied in a matter-of-fact tone, "Well, babe, you want to write, you want to help people, so are you going to trust God and move forward or find a reason it won't work?"

At that moment, God recruited Matt as part of my training team. He used my husband to remind me I was made for more and that He had a purpose for me. Like any good fighter, I listened to my husband because he was right. I needed to trust God, and if this was the road He chose for me to make a difference in people's lives, He would equip me. However, that didn't come easy. I am very familiar with my skills and strengths. It would be easy for me to get a job in ministry. But changing careers in a competitive field that I partake in but have no formal training needed to be made very clear. So, after praying, little signs started to pop up confirming this call. Signs like my doctor asking, "Have you ever considered helping women reclaim their health and stay on track with their health goals? You're an inspiration."

Or my favorite coach asking during class, "Have you ever thought of coaching? You would make a great coach."

But the voice that carried the most weight was my pastor. From the pulpit, he said, "Don't stay stuck where you are because of fear. You have so much more in you to give, to help others and impact people for the kingdom. If He is calling you, won't he equip you?"

That is all I needed to hear, and I set out to become a personal trainer and CrossFit coach.

The vision was much bigger than I could explain. Obstacles filled the road all along the way—caring for my father on his deathbed, receiving news that I had a rare lung disease and lymphoma, the pandemic, and navigating the children through the unknown.

Day and night, I fought to keep up with my studies. I was exhausted most days and lucky to retain anything I read. Crying myself to sleep, I would ask God, "What is your purpose for all this at once? I can't keep up. I am tired. Did you really ask this of me?"

Every day, my physical strength continued to dissipate due to the illness (others still didn't know about) wreaking havoc on my body. My dad was dying. I needed to be strong for him, my children, and Mom. I needed him to see me smile so he was not worried and would pass in peace. So, I pushed through each day and cried each night. I had the mental capacity of a squirrel and became emotionally numb.

My focus shifted to finishing school and getting to work—that's it. I disliked depending on my husband or being a financial burden.

A few months later, the big exam arrived. Again, my anxiety flew high, and I grew sick with fear. What if I failed?

I scrolled through my phone and read a text from my mom: *Julie, you need to have faith. I mean, you have faith that God has your soul but not your best interest. If He wants this for you, it will be yours, and if not, He has other plans for you. Don't you believe He has laid plans for you? He guides your feet; your steps are not your own.*

As usual, Mom was right, and I was left to think. I had been through so much and kept my eye on the goal the whole time. But what had I learned in the process? Was I trusting the Lord? That night, I went to bed and prayed for peace. Scripture says,

> "*We can make our plans,*
> *but the LORD determines our steps.*"
> *(Proverbs 16:9 NLT)*

We don't always know why we face the trials or obstacles we do. We won't always have peace in the transitions (those are uncomfortable places). Still, if we take our eyes off the expected outcome and surrender to God's process, we will discover deeper peace and understanding.

I let go and said, "God, I know what I know. You do what you do. If this was in your plan, guide my hands, and if not, give me peace."

Today, I am a trainer, and my accomplishments were not in the certifications but in walking through the process and trusting God in the unknown. Sometimes, we must fight the voices in our heads, lay down our pride, and listen for the still, small voice to guide and grow us through the process.

Reflection: Are you drowning in the process because your eyes are glued to the outcome? Read and meditate on Psalm 16:9. You can make all the plans you want, but God's plan for you is final. He has ordered your steps, and you need to trust the process no matter how difficult or painful it seems. In the process, you develop strength, character, and a deeper understanding of God's presence.

Prayer: Father God, I don't always understand why. I don't always trust the process. Please help me feel your peace and grow in the process you have before me. Please help me trust your Word over my knowledge. Let there be a testimony for me to share your goodness in my life.

In Jesus name, Amen

Investigate

"The journey is never all rainbows and butterflies...PRs and podium finish...I wish it were, but that's not reality."
– Dana Movsessian

In the world of competitive sports, there is a winner and a loser. If you are an athlete, you always hope to be the winner. The same holds true in combat sports. No fighter enters the ring or cage hoping for a loss, yet they know when they enter the arena, only one will win. Nothing feels better to a competitor than taking the win. It's why they train, the reason they make sacrifices and push themselves to limits normal people would not dream of. However, we forget the losses are just as important. Loss is the breeding ground for growth and change.

While scrolling through Facebook, I read my coach's long, heartfelt post, birthed from failure after a lifting competition. "I failed myself...and that is the disappointing moment. Not missing the lifts, but quitting on myself..." (Dana Movsessian).

Dana is my fitness coach and one of the most inspiring women I know. She reminded me that I could be a mom and still be an athlete, that I could set goals for my health and have fun crushing them. She reminded me of how good it felt to defy the odds and set an example to my boys of healthy living (and competition). Dana is a tough coach who pulls no punches and expects her athletes to grow as athletes and humans.

Dana always stands in our corner, pushing us harder, faster, and heavier. But just as hard as she pushes us, she celebrates our wins and grounds us. Quitting is never an option. So, imagine my surprise when I came across that post.

Athletes are cut from a different cloth. We are wired to win, and winning comes at a price. We train hard, play hard, fail hard, and respond to failure just as hard.

When we set our eyes on a goal, we stop at nothing to ensure we accomplish that goal, and this mindset becomes our life mantra. We DON'T QUIT. We don't quit on the process, the goal, the dream, and never on ourselves.

But sometimes, life hands us obstacles, pain after pain, uncertainty after uncertainty, causing us to stop dead in our tracks and second-guess everything we know and believe. When things turn upside down around us and nothing makes sense, it does not matter how we are wired. We all do the same thing: question who we are and what we are made of.

We even question who God is and why He would allow such pain, and guess what? That's okay! Because we are human. So ask, cry, and walk away from the barbell of life, but don't quit.

Because, as Dana said, life is not "all rainbows and butterflies... PRs and podium finishes."

We will have trouble. We will doubt, cry, and feel weak, helpless, and angry. Athletes will even freeze at the bar, mat, or wherever we perform. But we can't quit.

Scripture says,

> "*When you pass through the waters,*
> *I will be with you,*
> *and the rivers will not overwhelm you.*
> *When you walk through the fire,*
> *you will not be scorched,*
> *and the flame will not burn you.*"
> *(Isaiah 43:2 CSB)*

Not *if* we pass through waters but when. Not *if* we walk through fire but when. When we face challenging and impossible things, we must remember God is in them. When we feel alone, we must trust that God is in that lonely, defeated place with us.

Quitting is walking away from the bar or mat and never picking it up again. Quitting on ourselves is lying in defeat, allowing depression, anxiety, and fear to have their way, and succumbing to the darkness of failure. Quitting on God is believing He is no longer in control, bowing out, and walking away from our faith.

God said He would be with us, not maybe, but will be, and He does not lie. So yes, we feel the pain of disappointment. We face hardship, challenges, and doubt, but we are never alone in them.

So, we missed the lift. Get back behind the bar. So, we missed a tackle and threw a fight. We stopped writing, singing, praying, and believing. Lick those wounds, shake off the pride, and get back to the grind, allowing God to pave the way and heal our wounds.

Reflection: Time to investigate. Are you struggling with defeat? Is there something that has you bound in the "Why me, Lord? When will this stop?" Have you walked away from a dream? A goal? Review Isaiah 43:2 and reflect on its words. Allow it to penetrate your soul. Print it out, post it where you can see it, and say it daily. What is the fire you're walking through? Is it work? God is with you. Is it your marriage? God is with you. Is it a tragedy? God is with you. You will get through it, and you're not alone. Don't quit.

Prayer: Heavenly Father, you alone gave me life. It is your breath in my lungs and your Spirit in my heart. Please breathe life into the dead places of my heart. Revive my Spirit so that I may feel your presence in my pain. Strengthen me in my weaknesses and give me new hope. Thank you for always being with me, even if I don't feel you. Thank you for never quitting on me.

In Jesus' name, I pray. Amen.

Reposition

"It ain't about how hard you can hit. It's about how hard you can get hit and keep moving forward."
— Adonis Johnson

I love movies based on true stories. One of my favorites is *Cinderella Man*. Taking place during the Great Depression, this movie shows the reality of hardship, pain, and loss while capturing the essence of what it means to persevere. In one scene, Mae Braddock shows up to a fight to remind her husband (James) that they win fights together. Then she states, "Maybe I understand, some, about having to fight. So you just remember who you are" (Renee Zellweger, Mae Braddock, *Cinderella Man*). Unleashing all she sees in her husband, she ends with, "You are a hero to your children and the champion of my heart."

In a moment of fear and doubt, she chose to align herself with hope and love. She had faith and grit and stayed persistent, and she inspired me to do the same. Although we are not in the Great Depression, I felt a connection with her character. Like in some parts of the movie, I was watching myself.

I remember a time when my job was depleting me physically and emotionally and didn't pay the bills. A season where the children were acting out, being demanding, and testing boundaries. In constant overdrive, I would deal with children's school mishaps, reprimanding and teaching, yet feeling like I failed at loving. Every night, I was alone in bed, fighting tears because my husband worked nights, and I felt like a single parent all over again.

The walls were closing in on me, leaving me trapped in defeat and frustration. My pain, masked by control, became the armor I wore to protect me from more disappointment. Yet the stress continued to climb, and my home was more conducive to a fighting arena than a home. My marriage grew distant, and I grew cold, dutifully going through my responsibilities. I hated waking up every morning suffocating under the weight of failed expectations. This was not a mountaintop season for me, just one of the many valleys I walked through.

"From glory to glory. We can go from mountaintop to mountaintop." That sentence made me feel as though there was something wrong with me or my faith. Though the phrase is meant to encourage and build faith, it can do the opposite to those walking the valley.

It is misleading to expect that we will go from "glory to glory" and not face problems, experience turmoil, and walk through suffering. Victories are achieved by winning battles. Underdog stories are about people overcoming the odds when everything is stacked against them. And believers have a road map of how to navigate these trying times.

Countless stories of conflict pepper the Bible. Stories of tragedy, heartbreak, depression, anxiety, fear, and grief paved the way for us believers to follow. So why do we expect different in our current life? How do we hope to have David's faith, Paul's impact, and Ether's favor without going through our own fires? If only mountaintop experiences filled the Bible, why would we need a comforter, redeemer, or savior?

Truth is simple: we will walk through valleys as much as we glory on the mountaintop, and there is nothing wrong with that. How we handle the valley is what matters.

Roger Crawford says it best: "Being challenged in life is inevitable, being defeated is optional." Regardless of our pain, we don't have to live in defeat. The Spirit of God lives inside us. Therefore, we have access to His peace, comfort, and love. Even when we do not feel His presence, He is there.

Hebrews 10:35-36 (NIV) says, "So do not throw away your

confidence; it will be richly rewarded. You need to persevere so that when you have done the will of God, you will receive what he has promised."

While in the valleys, we have a choice. We can fight our own battles while our confidence and faith get shaken and feel defeated, or we can choose to hope in our creator, remembering and believing that God is by our side. He gives us strength to get through whatever storm we face. We can persist, and when we do, He will award us that which He promised us.

God will elevate us to the mountaintop, but we must be willing to reposition ourselves from fear, exhaustion, and weariness to a place of letting go and trusting God in our pain. When we choose to trust God, we begin to see mountains move and storms calm.

Reflection: Are you overwhelmed by the obstacles popping up and just want to quit? Revisit Hebrews 10:35-36 and hold it to your situation. Where is your confidence shaken? What is slowly taking your trust away from the Lord, causing you to want to give up? Take that fear and uncertainty and place it at His feet. Be still, and put your trust and hope in the Lord over the fear standing before you. Hold on to the promise He gave you, and when things feel heavy (as they will), take a position of worship. Let the song in your heart permeate your soul and give you peace as you persevere through this time.

Prayer: Heavenly Father, I don't know why I face the hardships I do. I don't want to quit, I don't want to stop trusting in you, but I get tired. I feel alone in battle, alone in thought, and alone in prayer. Lord, give me a song to praise you to fuel my Spirit and keep me strong. Give me a promise to hold on to as I place my trust in you daily. Lord, fill my atmosphere with your presence so that I may not feel alone but tangibly feel you with me.

In Jesus' name, I pray. Amen.

ROUND 5

Ground and Pound

Hiding the Blow

"The trauma said, 'Don't write these poems.
Nobody wants to hear you cry
about the grief inside your bones.'"
— Andrea Gibson, *The Madness Vase*

The stands fell deathly quiet. Both teams knelt, waiting as medics ran out on the field, and like a loved one seeing their fighter hit the mat in a knockout, a terrified mother stood behind the ropes, helpless, holding her breath and fighting the tears in her eyes.

I stared into my camera lens at the football player lying motionless on the field. "Lord, please let him be okay," I whispered, and a moment later, he stood on his feet with a coach on each side. The teams and audience clapped as he slowly walked off the field, and like that, the game ended.

I joined the scared mother on the sidelines and waited for our boys to come off the field. Her son approached us last, steaming mad, refusing to acknowledge us as we asked if he was okay and expressed concern. "I'm fine. Cheap shot that cost us the game. Just drop it," he barked, walking to the changing room. I encouraged his mom, and my son and I headed out. All night, I played that moment over in my head.

Kneeling on the sidelines with a zoomed-in camera, I caught the action shot that laid the young varsity player out on the field. A player on the opposite team had run in close and grabbed his jersey by the back collar, pulling him back as another player tackled him from the side, bringing him to the ground. He was right; it was a cheap shot, a dirty play. But it was football, and it was not his fault. He could not have seen that coming. Yet he carried that loss personally.

That was one of the best games I saw the football players play all year. Neither team had scored the entire game until the last nine seconds when he took that blow. They played well and should have been proud, but that hit changed the outcome in his eyes. They lost, and in his eyes, it was his fault.

Later that evening, my son explained how the teen was a varsity player helping the JV team. He was embarrassed (ashamed, really) that he "let down the team" with what he called "a rookie mistake."

I sat down, pulled the images from the game, and showed them to Ethan. "From where I was standing, there was no way he would have seen that coming. He didn't let anyone down, and he should not carry the shame of loss on his shoulders. He played well. You all did," I explained.

How often in the field of life do we take blows that knock us down, leaving us paralyzed? Trauma haunts us, yet we walk off our field, say "cheap shot," and try to move on from the pain and shame we hide.

How often do the voices in our heads overwhelm us with, "No one cares about the pains of our past; people have bigger problems," or play back the trauma, questioning whether we deserved what we were handed?

The enemy uses silence to bind us in shame, pain, and misery, separating us from the truth of God's Word and healing. Silence leaves us alone with the ghosts of our past, jeopardizing the hope of our future. I love how Andrea Gibson (*The Madness Vase*) wrote it out.

> "But my bones said, 'Tyler Clementi jumped
> from the George Washington Bridge
> into the Hudson River convinced
> he was entirely alone.'
> My bones said, 'Write the poems.'"

If we hide behind false healing, promises, or ideals, we isolate ourselves to deal with the pain we were never meant to experience alone.

Psalm 25:2 (NIV) tells us:

> *"I trust in you;*
> *do not let me be put to shame,*
> *nor let my enemies triumph over me."*

We may not be able to trust man with our heart or healing, but we can trust God. We can cry to Him and allow Him to guide our steps to healing and redemption.

So, whatever pains your soul in private, whatever monster is silencing you and keeping you from true healing, expose it under God's Word and trust in the Lord to restore you fully.

Reflection: Are you walking in false happiness, worried that the undercurrent of shame, anger, resentment, or pain will rip you away from reality? No matter what you do, these past pains continue haunting your present life, crippling you in ways you never expected. Where is your trust? Is it in a therapist alone? Is it in yourself? Or in no one at all? Reflect on the words in Psalm 25:2 and trust the Lord will go before you and guide you through your healing.

Prayer: Lord, today, I face the pains of my past and give them to you. Please help me release them and trust that you and you alone will restore my broken places. Please visit me the way only you can and touch my heart so that I may know you are guiding me through the healing process. I pray that you give me the scripture to stand on. Line up the right people, tools, and coping skills to help me defeat the hidden monsters. I pray for peace as you walk through this journey with me.

In Jesus' name, I pray. Amen.

Rage Out

"Don't spend time beating a wall, hoping to transform it into a door."
— Coco Chanel

Channeling all my frustration into one target, I wind up and jab...jab...left hook. Each hit of the bag sends adrenaline coursing through my veins. Moving in, showing no mercy, I keep pounding the bag like an enemy trying to take me down. Another three jabs and a hook. The heavy bag swings toward me with each blow. I continue swinging back at my silent opponent.

There is nothing like pounding on a punching bag to release some pent-up stress or anger. As a child, I was known to finish fights protecting those I love. As a teenager, I handled my stress or frustration by punching pillows, mattresses, or even walls. I had a short fuse and a hot temper, so it didn't take much to make my head spin. However, I approached most of life's obstacles the same way. I would hit them head-on, smashing through them, doing whatever it took to beat them, yet taxing myself, fighting fights that were not meant for me.

Many Christians are doing the same thing. Like an unchecked teenager, they smash through obstacles head-on, stopping at nothing if it threatens or hinders the promise lying before them.

Some of these "obstacles" present more like brick walls. Yet despite the wall's strength, we continue smashing at it relentlessly, hoping the situation in front of us changes. When our attempts fail, we lie on the floor in defeat, spinning our wheels in exhaustion while we think of ways to change what we can't control.

We are not responsible for others' actions, nor can we change the words spoken. Whether we are in the middle of a family feud, severed friendship, or parenting challenges, we must come to terms with the fact we cannot change the outcome of someone else's actions.

We can't change the words exchanged by fighting with friends, family, or loved ones. We can't control or change the hurt caused by our children's decisions as they navigate life.

However, we are responsible for our actions. We can control the fiery darts we toss at people (especially our children or family). Just because we feel hurt, angry, resentful, or frustrated doesn't mean we should spread the toxic behavior. Reacting from a place of hurt or pain only scars the people we love. It teaches our children it's okay to bruise the ones we love and passes that behavior on to the next generation. That does not have to be the story of our children or grandchildren. We can choose to forgive and grow from each challenge. We can set boundaries and watch our tongue in response to others.

> *"For the one who wants to love life*
> *and to see good days,*
> *let him keep his tongue from evil*
> *and his lips from speaking deceit."*
> *(1 Peter 3:10 CSB)*

1 Peter says if we want to see good days, we should keep our tongue from evil and our lips from speaking deceit. If we want to enjoy life and the days we have here, we need to hold our tongues.

This does not mean we can't speak our piece or that we should be pushovers. Instead, it means thinking before we speak and doing it with integrity. It means preventing the passion of frustration from building inside and leaking out in our words and actions, prohibiting others' actions from affecting family, friends, coworkers, and our children, and dictating how we respond because our words are our own. What we say matters, and though we can't control someone else's mouth, we can set boundaries to protect ourselves from toxic people and control our actions.

Reflection: Are you banging your head against a wall, hoping it will become a door? Are you trying to change the outcome of something out of your control? Are you anxious and unable to sleep because your head is spinning and you can't change the things lying before you? The scripture in Peter says that if you want to love life and see good days, you must keep your tongue from evil and your lips from speaking deceitfully. Write down a list of your frustrations. Is it people, work, family, or yourself? Is the list comprised of things you can control? If not, how are you responding to them? Take time to process what is triggering you to live a less-than-happy lifestyle, and if it's not yours to hold, let it go.

Prayer: Heavenly Father, thank you so much for your Word. Please reveal the walls in my life that are not mine to fight through. Help me see the areas that cause incredible frustration and cause me to live unsettled and on edge. Help me establish healthy boundaries and guide my tongue so I may see happier days and the fruit of your love.

In Jesus' name, I pray. Amen.

Fired Up

"If you can sit with your pain, listen to your pain and respect your pain—in time you will move through your pain."
– Bryant McGill, *Simple Reminders*

Making eye contact with my mom, I said, "Don't say a word. I don't want Dad or the kids to know. I'll tell the others after Dad passes. I don't want him worried about me."

That was a November I will never forget. The month my dad passed, I also got diagnosed with a rare lung autoimmune disorder and lymphoma.

The searing pain of fear and uncertainty hit deep, crippling me as I thought of my children's and spouse's futures. So much weighed on my mind. I wasn't ready to see the fear in my children's eyes. I didn't want to die or think about their life without me. I did not want them to feel the pain of losing a parent while they were processing the loss of their loved grandfather. And I didn't want pity from friends, family, or church members.

I would like to say I was a good girl and prayed, worshipped, read my Bible, and got better. But in reality, I questioned God, got angry, prayed, worshipped, screamed at God, cried, said sorry, and did it all over again. Like a boxer relentlessly hitting the bag over and over in a fit of rage until their knuckles are bleeding and searing with pain, I cried out to God with fear and grief for days and nights.

"Why would you allow this? Can't you see the pain it is causing my family? Can't you see their fear and mine? What is the lesson in this? Please don't let them grow up without me by their side." Finally, I said, "Lord, I can't do this. I am tired and too sick. Please give me the strength." I finally surrendered to the fact that nothing was within my control and trusted God was with me. Scripture says:

"The LORD is close to the brokenhearted
and saves those who are crushed in spirit."
(Psalm 34:18 NIV)

When you have watched life slip through a loved one's eyes and then faced your mortality, you have to make a choice: exercise the faith we speak so often about or walk away. Exercising faith means trusting in the unseen, trusting in the Lord, and believing that even when our Spirit is crushed, He is with us.

My process was messy and unrefined. But it was also healing and beautiful. I learned to sit in the pain and uncertainty and fully trust the Lord as He guided me through each day (or, at times, each minute). It taught me that even though my pain was deep and I could barely choke out a song, I didn't have to say a word. My Spirit was already crying out. In those moments, His Spirit washes over the place we are in and brings us comfort.

No one knows why we face pains and challenges (some more than others) the way we do. But regardless of what we face, our creator remains close to the brokenhearted. A Father who washes over us to bring us comfort in our deepest and darkest moments.

Reflection: Where are you mentally, emotionally, spiritually? Are you feeling shattered, lonely, and plagued with uncertainty? Are you asking God why? Reflect on Psalm 34:18. God is with you even when you are shattered or brokenhearted. When you don't have the strength, He does. He saves the crushed in Spirit.

Prayer: Heavenly Father, it's hard to let go of the people I love most. It's harder to release control of my own will for my life. I often feel I know what is best for me, but sometimes I fall short. I ask that you reveal yourself to me in this shattered world. Please draw near to my loneliness when I desperately need to feel your presence. Strengthen me by your Spirit and guide me out of my brokenness.

In Jesus' name, I pray. Amen.

Tap Out

"The activity of worrying keeps you immobilized."
– Wayne Dyer

Rocky is another one of my favorite underdog movies. This classic provides a small glimpse of how hard a fighter trains to master their skill, and they did a great job portraying what it takes to win physically and mentally. Rocky relentlessly trained, pushing his body past normal capacity as he adapted to the unconventional training method. He could have tapped out with exhaustion and pain, but he didn't. He chose to endure the pain, preparing both mentally and physically to outsmart his opponent.

In combat sports, you can lose by tapping out or getting beat down by your opponent. I have never been in the cage, but watching a fight, I get just as fired up. Something in me snaps when I see my fighter taking blow after blow. I scream and yell (as if he can hear me), "Get up, duck, block, punch…"

But if he gets trapped and locked down to the mat, my heart drops. "Oh, God, no…don't tap out! You can do it."

Flashbacks flood my mind of me squaring off with my brother in our living room and searing pain shooting through my arm while my brother pinned my arm to my back and my face to the floor. Every time I moved, his grip tightened, and the pain sharpened until I was forced to tap out. So, when I see a fighter rendered useless, I feel for them.

Tapping out in combat sports means a fighter held in a submission hold taps the mat or their physical body, admitting defeat, ending the fight.

The thought of my opponent having me in such a painful hold, forcing me to submit to them or experience grave consequences, makes me sick. I was annoyed I had to submit to my brother, let alone anyone else. I can't imagine what fighters feel at that moment as thousands of people watch them being brought under their opponent's submission.

Yet we spend our days and even weeks immobilized by circumstances. We fight fights that are not ours and worry about problems we can't control. Day in and day out, we choose to tap out, allowing the enemy to take the victory of our joy and peace.

We don't have to tap out. James 4:7 (NKJV) tells us, "Therefore submit to God. Resist the devil and he will flee from you."

First, we must hold our circumstances to the truth of God's Word. Submit to God and His way (no matter how uncertain it seems). Resist fighting against the "devils" of our circumstances. Fight against the need to control the situation and the lack of trust in our God and resist the temptation to walk away under pressure. Trust that as you "draw near to God…He will draw near to you" (James 4:8 NKJV).

Reflection: Are you in danger of tapping out? Are you in an impossible situation where you feel you will lose no matter what you do? Read James 4:7-8 and ask yourself where to submit to the Lord. You can't hold on to a lack of trust and expect to walk in victory.

Prayer: Heavenly Father, sometimes my circumstances seem impossible. Occasionally, I feel trapped, with no options, and want to tap out. Please reveal where I need to submit myself to you and walk in your peace. Help me resist the devils I face as I continually draw near to you.

In Jesus' name, I pray. Amen.

ROUND 6

Gluten for Punishment

Run the Course, Not Your Mouth

"Don't mix bad words with your bad mood. You will have many opportunities to change a mood, but you will never get the opportunity to replace the words you spoke."
– Unknown

I heard a saying on the playground growing up: "Sticks and stones may break my bones, but words will never hurt me."

I quickly learned that was not true. Other girls mocked and made fun of me for not having the right clothes, haircut, or makeup. The wounds I bore secretly cut far deeper than a black eye or bruised knees. Their harsh words left me feeling inadequate, unattractive, and unvalued. Reckless childhood words left wounds that scarred me for years, and as a result, I became a professional stonewaller who knew how to shatter anyone's soul in minutes with only words. I did it to "protect" myself from being hurt by others.

Over time, I had trouble with my family, marriage, and children, all because I could not keep my tongue in check and often took out my anger on the ones I loved most.

Proverbs 12:18 (NIV) says, "The words of the reckless pierce like swords, but the tongue of the wise brings healing."

Pre-fight interviews are often where fighters smack-talk their opponent, making comments in hopes of getting under their skin enough that they cause them to be less focused come fight night. A fighter who can't think clearly is blind to what is coming in the ring because they are drawing from raw emotion and not a level head. A fighter can be dangerous in that place. Full of uncontrolled rage they can severely hurt or, worse, kill their opponent.

The same holds true in day-to-day life. Running our mouths out of anger and frustration catalyzes pain and destruction. It will pierce through the hearts of people we target and cause wounds we can't undo (killing their self-esteem).

If we have already done some damage, the good news is that we can undo the hurt we caused, starting with owning our mistakes. Acknowledging the pain we caused is the first step (whether we agree with how they feel or not). Telling them we are sorry for the pain we caused is the second step. The last step is telling the person we love that we will try our best to choose words more diligently, reminding them we won't always be perfect and will get it wrong sometimes but will continue trying. My husband and I had an "emergency phrase" that told me I was close to blowing a fuse. When I heard the phrase, "Babe, it's time to get to the gym," I knew I needed a timeout or I was going to cause damage to my children. Coming up with a mutual code while neither party is in a bad mood can help identify when a temper needs to be stifled and stop a war before it happens.

We can also operate with self-control and use wisdom before we speak. We can humble ourselves, choose not to react in a situation, and pray, ask God to help us respond with wisdom and grace, and then watch as God heals the wounds and problems we face. We don't always need to be right, especially at the sacrifice of someone else's heart. We will lead a more peaceful life if we run the course and ask God for wisdom instead of running our mouths.

Reflection: Have you been a victim of words that left you broken? Or maybe you are the one with the sharp tongue used to defend a hidden broken heart. Read Proverbs 12:18 and ask yourself this: Am I responding to situations out of frustration and impulse, or am I responding with a clear head and mind? Is God in the response, or am I justifying actions I will later regret? Then, ask God to reveal the cause of your delivery and give you the wisdom to change your behavior.

Prayer: Lord, it is no surprise that I can't control my tongue. Yet you love me anyway. Please shed light on where I need to grow. Help me to hold my tongue and not react when I am in challenging positions. Help me hear your voice and feel your prompting, guiding me to a better way of handling conflict. If my heart is wounded by someone's toxic words, I pray you sweep into the broken places and heal them with your truth and love. Father, let my words bring you honor and glory in all areas of my life.

In Jesus' name, I pray. Amen.

Caged

"Anger and bitterness rob you of peace, not your enemy."
– Allene vanOirschot, *Daddy's Little Girl: A Father's Prayer*

Trapped behind the bulletproof wall, it lingers...
Anger
Hurt
Confusion.
Shattered,
by the prospect of freedom
false hope
Bitter
Alone
Silently battling to break free
From the internal cage that enslaved me.

Trauma does not respect age, race, or gender. Whether you experienced it as a child or adult, the outcome is the same. Something was taken from you, leaving you feeling useless, helpless, ashamed, alone, angry, disgusted, and even wanting to die. In the end, you are left building walls to a cage protecting what's left of your heart or dignity, trying not to become a victim again. But it's that very cage we build to protect us that destroys us.

I handed my friends some cash and watched them walk into the convience store. Cracking the passenger window a little more, I sat back in my seat and smoked a cigarette. Replaying the fight with my mom, I was lost in thought and didn't notice a man approach our car. "Hey, shorty, you got a smoke?"

Jumping up in my seat, I answered, "No," and rolled my eyes while leaning forward to roll up my window. In seconds, he reached through what was left open and grabbed my neck. Adrenaline kicked in, and I punched his arm as I reached for the handle to swing the door open (in an effort to knock him over). My friend hopped in the driver's seat and hit the gas, knocking him off me as she drove out of the parking lot.

I rubbed my neck and glanced behind me. The gold chain and heart pendant my father had given me were gone.

Heat washed over me, and I screamed, "Stop. Turn around. That thug has my necklace." But she refused. Instead, she drove to the police station. Anger coursed through my veins. I was mad at my mother for "causing my distraction." I was mad at my friends for not going back (even though they were protecting me). I was mad at the police for not trying to calm me down and not sending someone out fast enough to find the thief. I was mad at the world. From that night on, I had a solid hatred for men of my race, trust issues with friends, and a fractured relationship with my mother. Countless nights, I sat in my room raging out, punching mattresses (imagining people's faces who I felt deserved a beating), and screaming into pillows. With every victorious hand-to-hand combat, I imagined the bars of my cage grew stronger, as if tungsten surrounded by flame yet unscathed.

I trusted no one and would prove I could take care of myself.

Bitterness is an ugly root that burrows deep within our hearts. The more we experience disappointment, betrayal, and hurt, the deeper the root goes and the harder it is to eradicate.

At some point, we build a toxic bulletproof wall to keep others out while we remain trapped by pain and anger, never fully moving past shattered dreams and broken promises.

Enslaved to pain, we become the vessel that unintentionally poisons others with harsh words or cold distance, protecting our already broken hearts by refusing to allow anyone too close.

What has sitting behind our self-induced cage done for us? Nothing, except spread the toxicity of pain to others and breed resentment. Hebrews 12:14-15 (CSB) says, "Pursue peace with everyone, and holiness—without it, no one will see the Lord. Make sure that no one falls short of the grace of God and that no root of bitterness springs up, causing trouble and defiling many."

We need to pursue peace. It does not just fall on our lap. Hurt people hurt people, and regardless of the hurts we have faced, the Bible says we should pursue peace and holiness with everyone. Without that, they will not see the Lord. Think about that. As believers, we want to show this broken world the love of Christ. We want to give hope to a lost world. If we pursue peace in pain and trust God will make right our wrongs, we plant seeds of hope, love, and faith instead of bitterness and brokenness.

Reflection: Are you caged behind the pain of past hurts? Have those hurts caused you to hurt the people around you with a sharp tongue or short fuse? Reflect on Hebrews 12:14-15. How can you pursue peace in a world of hurt? Where can you step out and show God's love?

Prayer: Heavenly Father, the root of bitterness stems from my broken heart. I pray you touch my heart and fill me with your peace and presence. Please show me where I need to trust in you and let go of the angry or bitter root. Help me to show others who you are as I pursue your peace daily.

In Jesus' name, I pray. Amen.

Arm Bar

"Everyone must choose one of two pains:
The pain of discipline or regret."
– Jim Rohn

One afternoon, after a short yelling match, my brother and I started the usual smack-talking and shoving. He was getting on my nerves, and as usual, I was ready to shut him up with my fist.

As the oldest of three, I had my share of protecting my siblings and smacking around my younger brother (when he wanted to "prove" he was stronger than me). I prided myself in the fact that not only was I a girl, but I was a force to be reckoned with, and I was not going to let a boy take me out, not even my brother. But this day was different. As I advanced toward my brother to take him down, I found myself on the ground, unable to move with my arm held between his legs against his hip and torso in seconds. "Let go!" I shouted.

His smug, cold, confident tone told me I was in trouble. "How do you like me now, Julie? TAP OUT!"

Nobody likes to lose a fight, whether facing off with a sibling or in a cage in front of hundreds of people. When pride is on the line, we will stop at nothing to prove our strength and skill. Tapping out was not an option for me.

Pain seared through my elbow and arm, but I refused to give in. "NEVER, BRAT!"

My brother applied more pressure and taunted, "Move now. I DARE YOU."

Writhing in pain, I tried to bite one of his legs but couldn't get my teeth in far enough to do damage. More pain shot through my arm with each move I made, yet I refused to submit.

My younger sister watched it all happen. Panicked and desperate to help me, she started to cry. In between sobs, she screamed, "You're hurting her. Let go."

When that didn't work, she screamed louder. "You're going to break her arm. Stop it!"

Right on cue, our mother stomped up the stairs, shouting, "JULIE AND DAVID, you better not be fighting."

"Snitch," my brother whispered as he released me.

Barely able to move my arm, I stood to my feet and walked away. Not only was my brother teaching himself martial arts, but he taught me a lesson. Once my pride allowed, I asked him what he did to me.

"An arm bar. It could have broken your arm, but Mom came just in time."

No matter how good a fighter we may be, we will always have a weakness. If our opponent can identify that spot and move in undetected, we may (more often than not) lose.

The arm bar is a submission hold used in combat sports—I was lucky enough to escape with a minor injury. The hold keeps an opponent's arm in a lever-like position, hyperextended and usually against their body, creating an ungodly amount of pressure to the elbow joint, causing them to tap out. If the opponent chooses not to tap out, they risk tearing ligaments and tendons and breaking the bone.

A quick way to end a fight, right? Unless you are stubborn like me and would rather tear the ligaments and risk the break before submitting. That same stubbornness has us in a metaphoric arm bar.

What has us hyperextended and stuck, unable to move in life? Is it constantly putting in extra hours with no work-life balance? Maybe it's picking up balls that others continuously drop so "the team" doesn't look bad to the boss.

Have we been sideswiped by circumstances we can't control yet attempt to? Is the pressure so intense we are ready to tap out?

We don't have to live a life of hyperextension and pain. We don't have to be the yes man to coworkers, friends, or family. We must discipline our minds and bodies alike.

Galatians 6:2-5 (NIV) says, "Carry each other's burdens, and in this way you will fulfill the law of Christ. If anyone thinks they are something when they are not, they deceive themselves. Each one should test their own actions. Then they can take pride in themselves alone, without comparing themselves to someone else, for each one should carry their own load."

Sure, the scripture tells us to "carry each other's burdens," but the truth is many of us get stuck there. To be more like Christ, we need to serve more, do more, help more. That soon turns into overextending in all areas of life, causing us to burn out and feel frustrated, undervalued, overworked, and taken for granted.

But what about the part of the verse that says, "Each one should test their own actions. Then they can take pride in themselves alone, without comparing themselves to someone else, for each one should carry their own load"? (Galatians 6:4-5 NIV) Are we disciplined enough to search our hearts and ask why we overextend? Is there a motive behind what we are doing? Are we comparing ourselves to someone else or staying in our own lane? If we exercise self-evaluation of the heart while setting proper boundaries, not only will we hold others responsible for their load, but we can finally live in peace, removing ourselves from the pressure of that arm bar.

Reflection: What have you hyperextended? What is applying so much pressure in your life, you feel you might quit? Reflect on Galatians 6:2-5 and ask yourself what things can be released. Are you hyperextended because you are trying to please man or God? It's time to start disciplining yourself to say no and teach others to carry their weight. It's time to set boundaries in your life so you can live in more peace without the weight of unrealistic expectations and affirmation from man. It's time to free yourself from the pressure so you don't continue living in regret.

Prayer: Father, thank you for the heart to serve. Thank you for setting the example of love and sacrifice. Today, I ask that you reveal to me how to guard my time. Help me develop healthy boundaries so I do not grow weary under unnecessary pressure attempting to please man. Please bring clarity to my circumstances and give me the wisdom to apply my best.

In Jesus' name, I pray. Amen.

Bow

"Bowing is an expression of gratitude and respect.
In effect, you are thanking your opponent for giving
you an opportunity to improve your technique."
– Jigaro Kano

"Your God is an absent landlord," said a friend (we will call her Chelsey).

I nodded my head, understanding her pain but feeling like I was sucker punched in the gut and the wind was knocked out of me. I continued listening as she poured out the darkest thoughts plaguing her mind. This was not like her. She was strong, fierce, and independent. People respected her and looked up to her, yet in this moment, all I saw was pain.

"Listen," I said. "You're hurt and mad. I get it. But God has not left you. He is still with you even if you don't see him."

Fire flashed in her eyes, and she snapped, "Funny way of showing Himself, watching as I continue to help others while they stab me in the back. Watching as I give to countless and struggle to pay my own bills. Stand by while I try to mend our broken family, only to continue being hurt and betrayed. Why does he allow pain after pain, struggle after struggle? Why?"

"I don't know." I choked back tears. "But I am sorry for those that hurt and betrayed you. I don't know why you are the one under continuous fire. But I do know that God is with you even when you can't see Him. He sent me to stand with you. And I will always be here walking the high road with you."

In some martial arts cultures, bowing is a sign of respect to opponents' trainers and a sign of good intention. When your opponent bows back, they are showing you the same respect.

But not all opponents will bow. Not all fighters care about respecting you or the authority around the sport. What do we do when they are out for blood and we see it in their eyes?

We bow. Character is revealed best under pressure. Who we are in public reflects where we are in private, especially under pressure.

Maybe we have been beaten down by loss—loss of a job, loved one, or friend. Perhaps lingering insecurities from rejection and past pains plague us. Perhaps we see failure when we look in the mirror and feel we should be further in life than where we currently are.

We face insecurities, depression, sadness, doubt, and so on for countless reasons. Each one of those negative emotions or mental "instabilities" can be better known as our opponents in life. It becomes what we combat daily to keep face for others around us.

Here's the secret, though: We don't need to save face for an audience. We need to stay true to ourselves and trust in God.

So, when our opponent stands before us with fire in its eyes, waiting to take us out, do we shrink back in fear? No, we acknowledge its presence, stand firm in our training, and tell the enemy we will not surrender.

Galatians 2:20 (CSB) states, "I have been crucified with Christ, and I no longer live, but Christ lives in me. The life I now live in the body, I live by faith in the Son of God, who loved me and gave himself for me." Although our opponents are strong, God is stronger. It takes great faith to press into God in a silent battle.

Not giving up takes greater faith when everything feels hopeless and lost. But the Bible says, "I live by faith in the Son of God, who loved me and gave himself for me." God loved us enough to give his life for us. He won't just leave us high and dry in battle. Therefore, we must stop trying to do things in our strength and press into God. Every great warrior has a sensei (trainer), so we shouldn't be afraid to reach out to a counselor, pastor, or pastoral staff for prayer, support, and advice. Allow the people God placed in your life to lift and support you in your time of need.

Reflection: Are you in a silent battle? Are you falling apart in silence while trying to keep face in public? Read Galatians 2:20 and remember how much God LOVES YOU. Where does your faith lie? Is it in something fluid or planted in the Lord of creation?

Prayer: Heavenly Father, I am broken; fill me up while I rest in your presence. Please give me the strength to stand against the opponents haunting me. Surround me with people who hear from you to help strengthen me when I am afraid and defeated. Thank you for loving me enough to die for me. Now, help me live a life full of faith in you.

In Jesus' name, I pray. Amen.

ROUND 7

Danger Zone

The Toxic Call of Fear

"Have no fear of perfection—you'll never reach it."
– Salvador Dali

The ring announcer introduces the fighters competing on fight night. He will often ask questions like, how did you prepare for this fight? What did you think of your opponent's last fight? How did you strengthen your weakness?" These interviews bait the fighters to expose what their game plan is while attempting to strike fear in their opponent to throw them off their game. High school can be like the octagon. It's where hormones are high and tempers fly.

A place where we begin discovering who we are and what we are made of. We chase dreams, explore opportunities, and plan for our future. High school can be as wild and unpredictable as the octagon.

Students try to find their place within those four walls. Where do they fit? Are they good enough? So many questions haunt them as they try to prove their worth to their teachers and peers. I will never forget those years—those are the years that molded me into who I am today. We can say, "It's no big deal," or, "It's just high school." But truth be told, our lives are not much different. It's just a different set of walls.

We still want to be the best at work, validated or accepted by our peers (coworkers), we still want to make a difference in this world, and we are still afraid to fail.

As I drove my son to the football field for football cuts, he asked, "What if I'm not good enough? What if I don't have what it takes to make the team? What if I'm wasting your time?"

I placed my hand on his shoulder. "Ethan, you're not wasting my time. This is your time. Do you want this?"

"Yes, Mom, I just want to be great. I want to be the best."

I nodded. "Well, becoming the best starts with the willingness to fail and learn from your failure. David Goggins was afraid and suffered great anxiety. But he wanted to be a SEAL, and he did not stop until he was, no matter how many times he failed. If he is one of your inspirations, then fight like him. Stop being afraid of not being enough and train as hard as you can. Stay teachable, keep going above what's required, and you will achieve your greatness. Now, go have some fun."

It's so easy to get stuck in that mindset. The mindset that paralyzes us from moving forward or even trying at all. In our media-driven world, we are surrounded by people being put on blast, exposing failures and imperfections. We are surrounded by criticism and ridicule, or we measure our chapter one to someone else's finished book. In that sense, we are like high school kids, terrified to move forward and make a fool of ourselves. So, we get comfortable in dead dreams and shattered hopes.

But we don't have to live there. We just need to pursue the Lord and stay humble. If he placed a dream in our hearts, we must stop looking at someone else's version and focus on the one God gave us. If we fail, we figure out why, find a plan to help us improve, stay disciplined to the plan, and most importantly, stay teachable. Learn under someone else. Continue to remain teachable so we can grow.

Scripture says,

> *"In the same way, you who are younger, submit yourselves to your elders.*
> *All of you, clothe yourselves with humility toward one another, because,*
> *God opposes the proud*
> *but shows favor to the humble."*
> *(1 Peter 5:5 NIV)*

Don't be too proud to learn from someone who has gone before. God will honor our humility and raise us. Before we know it, our dreams will be reality.

Reflection: It's easy to give up on yourself and make excuses for why you still have unfinished business to attend to. Maybe you are too prideful to ask for help or afraid of failing. Failure only wins if you allow it. Failure is simply another chance to get it right and the opportunity to grow and learn under another who may be wiser than you. If you struggle to move past failing or ask for help, read 1 Peter 5:5.

Write down two or three people you know have the wisdom you need to grow where you are going. Reach out if you do not know anyone. Ask someone in leadership how you continue growing and follow up where they lead.

Prayer: Heavenly Father, failure keeps me in a state of broken dreams and shattered hopes. Help me to look at failure as an opportunity and to be humble enough to ask for help. Lord, I ask that everyone reading this may have a fresh fire burning within them and that it be unquenchable. I pray that you provide them with the guidance and wisdom they need to move forward. May they set up their discipline to move forward and not falter. May help come to those who need it and wisdom be received, and most of all, show your favor upon them as the dreams you gave them birth into reality.

In Jesus' name, I pray. Amen.

Scars of Disappointment

"Blessed is he who expects nothing, for he shall never be disappointed."
– Alexander Pope

"The interview went great. I'm now waiting for the second interview. I should hear back by the end of the week," I said to my best friend on the phone.

"I think you would be perfect for this position. I hope you get it. Keep me posted."

The words come bubbling out in excitement. "I can't believe I'm considering going back into full-time ministry. But I feel so alive. I can't wait to see what God has in store for me."

After two weeks of waiting, I received an e-mail stating that the church I had applied to reviewed my application but had decided to go a different route. I didn't get the job, and the betrayal stung. I was more than qualified and had plenty of experience, so why not me? Why didn't I even get the chance for another interview?

Life is full of disappointments, and if we have not had them, then we are not living. Disappointment happens when we have our hopes set on something important to us and are let down.

An athlete can be disappointed in their performance or loss in a game, a fighter disappointed with a match, a child disappointed in a parent's decision, a parent disappointed in their children's behavior, or a husband or wife disappointed in their marriage. We will all be let down at some time or another. The question is, how do we handle that disappointment? Do we dust off, accept it, and move on, or do we flirt with disaster and expect to come out unscathed?

When an athlete competes, they are expected to remain clean of drugs and or "enhancements" that can better their performance. The use of such things is considered cheating and a direct violation of the sport. However, many athletes choose to risk their titles and disqualification over facing the disappointment of failure.

That's a significant risk for someone who spends an extensive amount of time training to compete. Yet, without fail, we see athletes make the news from this type of disqualification all the time. They are left feeling the sting of regret and even greater disappointment for letting their fans down, but most importantly, themselves.

Avoiding the pain of disappointment by self-medicating (whether it be with sex, drugs, alcohol, shopping, or eating) may pacify us momentarily. But it will only set us up for defeat, same as the disqualified athlete. Putting hope in something fleeting will always cause greater disappointment. Instead, we need to trust in God. Not just our minds but our hearts. We need to remember He is for us, not against us, and resides in our discouragement.

Colossians 3:23-25 (NIV) says, "Whatever you do, work at it with all your heart, as working for the Lord, not for human masters, since you know that you will receive an inheritance from the Lord as a reward. It is the Lord Christ you are serving. Anyone who does wrong will be repaid for their wrongs, and there is no favoritism."

Whatever we are doing, do it clean. Work for that promotion for God Himself. When we serve our husbands, raise those kids, and train for God, we receive an inheritance from the Lord. Don't give up in the face of disappointment. Don't let disappointment alter your perspective. It may not always be easy to avoid the temptations of coping our way. But stay the course and trust that God will take care of the details; the wrongs we face will be made right. May we persevere and always strive to bring honor and glory to the Lord in our day-to-day life so He will raise us in time.

Reflection: Life's disappointments can derail you, and you forget who you serve and whose you are. Reread Colossians 3:23-25. No matter the circumstances you face, you serve a good God. If you struggle with health, continue serving Him in your daily activities. If you hope for a promotion, work like you are working for the Lord (because you are) and bring your company your best. If you need improvement in marriage and family, serve them as you do the Lord. It is not always easy. But you must trust that God will reward you for your faithfulness and take care of those wrongs.

Prayer: Lord, disappointment can be hard to deal with. It breaks my Spirit and causes me to doubt. I pray that I remember to bring it to you amid my disappointment, that I continue moving forward as if serving you, that I bring you glory even in my disappointment, and that I find favor in your eyes. I pray that you put all the pieces together for me and I find peace and victory in every circumstance.

I ask this in your mighty name, Jesus. Amen.

Ax Kick

"Anguish often causes us to physically crumple in on ourselves, literally bringing us to our knees or forcing us all the way to the ground. The element of powerlessness is what makes anguish traumatic. We are unable to change, reverse, or negotiate what has happened."
– Brené Brown, *Atlas of the Heart*

The ax kick is my favorite martial art kick. It is a great way to get an opponent off guard. We expect a front kick or side kick, but the ax kick is a vertical downward kick where the fighter kicks straight up, head height, and hammers his leg straight down on his target at the head or collarbone and shoulder. It is a swift, effective, and powerful move that leaves the opponent on their knees in seconds.

The day after Thanksgiving, I felt like I was on the receiving end of an ax kick. That week, I had to say goodbye to my father.

I was a daddy's girl, and even as an adult, I ensured everyone knew I was the princess. I loved my father with every fiber of my being. Why? Though he was not my biological father, he loved me no different than his own. He taught me to love and how to love the Lord.

Although we know our parents won't be around forever, I don't think we are ever fully ready to say goodbye. Nothing could have prepared me for the scream that escaped my mother's mouth when my father drew his last breath—a soul-shattering and all-consuming anguish in one breath. It was more than I could bear.

Overwhelming grief and denial hit me all at once when I had to call for a nurse to pronounce my father. At that moment, I felt empty, like my soul had left with his.

And just like that, all the colors in my life suddenly fell gray.

Good-intentioned people say clichés like "to be absent with the body is to be present with the Lord." But when we feel stripped of hope, love, and power over our circumstances, nothing they say makes it better; nothing anyone says can make it better.

We may be defeated and vulnerable, but we are not alone. This is where our relationship with God matters and where we discover what we are made of. Is our faith grounded deep, or is it shallow and unstable? Do we truly have a relationship with God or simply know of Him?

Job is one of the many godly men who show us what it means to be rooted in faith. The book of Job not only reveals that Job is not a "super Christian," meaning he does not hide his feelings, but it speaks of the pain, anguish, and suffering of a man who had and kept great integrity.

Job both questioned and trusted God in his suffering. In his darkest moments, he asked that his life be taken, and then he cried for mercy and held steadfast to hope in the Lord.

Job 14 illustrated his vulnerability, understanding of mortality, and yet strength in answering the Lord's call. But my favorite part of chapter fourteen is verses seven through nine (NIV):

> *"At least there is hope for a tree:*
> *If it is cut down, it will sprout again,*
> *and its new shoots will not fail.*
> *Its roots may grow old in the ground*
> *and its stump die in the soil,*
> *yet at the scent of water it will bud*
> *and put forth shoots like a plant."*

This verse reminded me of when we wanted to remove a shrub in our yard. My husband cut it down at the base after hours of trying to dig it out and getting nowhere. He thought that cutting through all those roots and then cutting it down to a stump would kill it and allow us to remove it later.

However, one month later, that stump had buds and new shoots.

I was amazed that after the amount of damage the shrub had taken (being dug, pulled, and cut down), it birthed new shoots.

This is because the roots gave it life. It fed the tree. The roots stayed intact, pulling energy from the sun, water, and soil. In time, it restored its broken body.

It is a beautiful portrait of how we should be with God. We should be rooted in him even when everything is falling apart. Even when we feel like Job and we want to die. Stay connected to our energy source. He will feed our souls, and new life will grow from the broken places.

Reflection: Heart check! Where are you emotionally? Are you checked out? Questioning why you are alive like Job? There is still hope for you. Read Job 12:7-9. Where are your roots? Are they running deep or easily pulled out of the ground, at risk of drying out and dying?

You can't see clearly in the all-consuming darkness. That's OK. If you can't see past the pain, seek counsel through a pastoral team that can walk alongside you. There is no shame or lack of faith in asking for help in times of darkness.

Prayer: Heavenly Father, thank you for always hearing me. Thank you for leaving me your Word, where I can access people who came before me. I can see their pain, struggle, and mourning but also your compassion and love for your people. Thank you for always being there amid my pain and suffering, even when I don't feel your presence.

Today, I ask that you touch the hearts of those struggling to see past the pain. I pray that you open their eyes and give them new hope. I pray that any lie the enemy whispers to them falls on deaf ears and that you restore the broken places in their hearts. Lord, speak to your people. If they are in need of council, speak to their Spirit and lead them to the right place or send them to the right person.

Thank you for the healing that is taking place in the broken hearts of your people.

In Jesus' name, I pray. Amen.

Grappling

"If you only do what is easy, you will always remain weak."
— Joyce Meyer, *Battlefield of the Mind*

While training one evening, my coach saw an opportunity to build my cardio strength, something I had told her I wanted. We did burpees, box jumps, and lifts. Exhausted after the third round, I said to myself, "I only have two rounds left. I just need to push through. Maybe I'll scale back on the burpees so I can move through the rounds quicker."

I swore my coach was a mind reader. At the bottom of my burpee, she stood right next to me, and as I popped up, without hesitation, she said, "You're doing four more than what's on that board."

I caught my breath and said, "Four more? Are you trying to kill me?"

She walked away. "Do you want to get stronger or stay where you are?"

Once again, she saw something I did not see in myself. Once again, she was right. I could do the hard things. But I had to decide at that moment: Would I listen to the noise in my head telling me to quit when things were hard and uncomfortable, or would I persevere?

People in combat sports like martial arts, MMA, or boxing share a common goal. They train hard to achieve a certain level of greatness. With a relentless hunger and drive, they chase after the belt (and the reputation that comes with it) that says they are skilled in their art.

This road requires grit, determination, and perseverance. Many start the journey, but few see the result. Training requires time, sacrifice, and a willingness to work in and out of the ring, mat, or cage. Anyone who wants a belt must be disciplined enough to train hard, work harder, and eat right. Most importantly, they trust and listen to the coaches guiding them to greatness and learn from their defeats.

It sounds simple enough; however, when the time comes to face the pain of lifting more weight, running faster or longer, or eating that extra piece of cake, what is our response? Do we do what's easy, or do we do what's hard, making us stronger?

Every day, garbage enters our minds that can pull us from our purpose. We all grapple with doubts, insecurities, fears, and frustration. We all have that inner fight where we question whether to scale back or face the discomfort and push forward.

Whether I am training my body and fatigue tries to keep me from my goals, or I am faced with a circumstance, the battle always starts and ends in my mind.

Ephesians 6:10 begins the armor of God, telling us to actively put on every piece of armor. Although the whole chapter is great, this simple sentence packs a punch: "Finally, be strong in the Lord and his mighty power" (Ephesians 6:10 NIV).

Simply put, we do not have the strength to face these things alone. We won't always have the mental or physical capacity to push through particular circumstances. So, are we drawing our strength from ourselves or utilizing the Lord's strength?

Reflection: Where are you struggling? Are you doing what is easy to avoid the discomfort and headaches of doing what is hard? Are you depending solely on your strength and your resources, or are you trusting and drawing from the strength of the Lord? Ephesians 6:10 reminds you that the source of your strength is the Lord. Reflect on that statement.

Prayer: Father, today I ask you to quiet the noise in my mind. Allow me to hear your voice, and show me where I need to draw from your strength. If the chatter does not stop, I pray you send someone to speak into my life as I grow in your strength. Give me peace in uncertainty and clarity in the storm.

In Jesus' name, Amen.

ROUND 8

Interception

Headlock

"Don't set yourself on fire trying to keep others warm."
— Penny Reid, *Beard in Mind*

As the oldest growing up, I was raised to protect my siblings at all cost. Whenever we went for walks, walked to school, or went on bike rides, I had eyes on them to make sure they were safe. If they got beat on the playground, I was sent to vindicate the wrong. If they were getting picked on in school, I would run to their aid. I was never the one to start the fight, but I had no problem finishing it. My training ground was grappling with the neighborhood boys. Some trained in karate, and I loved the sweet victory of taking them down in their own sport. Until I couldn't.

"I won't quit. I can't," I said as I desperately tried to escape. Thoughts of my siblings and my mother (who trusted me to protect them) flooded my head. "It can't end like this. I have to win."

At age fifteen, in a usual grappling challenge (to prove I was stronger than the guys), I quickly and unexpectedly found myself under the submission of a neighborhood boy (we'll call him Nate).

Nate's arm wrapped around my neck and head, and his other arm pinned me to the ground, leaving me helpless under the weight and pressure of his body. Unable to move outside of frantically flailing my limbs, I could not escape. With each feeble attempt to break free, he tightened his grip like a boa constrictor wrapped around its prey, slowly squeezing until it stopped moving.

When I began to fatigue, Nate slyly said, "This is a headlock. I won't let go, and you won't get out until you tap out."

Defeat was bitter that evening. He outwitted me, and I was furious. But not at him, at myself for not being enough and for failing at the role entrusted to me. It meant that if I lost to a friend, I could lose to others, leaving my siblings without a protector.

I dragged this childhood fight through my adult life like an unseen snare. Poachers use snares to catch animals in the wild. They are typically long pieces of wire tied to a stationary object, like a big tree, with a loop at the other end. When a poacher sets up their snare, they select the size and quantity of wire to guarantee success for the size of the prey they are hunting. The setup is simple yet deadly. They start by leaving the loop dangling just low enough off a branch that when the passing animal passing walks into it, the loop slips right over its head. As the animal travels forward or tries to escape, the snare tightens around their neck until the animal eventually dies of asphyxiation.

Animals too large for the trap can rip the snare off the base, traveling with it attached to its body. If left unnoticed or untreated, these animals die due to serious infection or poor circulation. Like an elephant that accidentally walked through a small snare, I grew up under the unhealthy thought patterns of always having to prove my worth. Fighting fights that were not mine to prove my strength and wounding others with words, showing they could not hurt me with theirs. I continued to carry that snare while it slowly tightened, creating wounds so bad it infected every area of my life. Some of us may still be carrying it—the snare of codependency.

When people say codependent, we often think of a man or woman who can't function in daily life without someone giving them affirmation or someone struggling with substance abuse.

Although both of these scenarios are true, codependency goes deeper than that. It can sneak into our daily situations and affect us on multiple levels: "Codependents, busy taking care of others, forget to take care of themselves, resulting in a disturbance of identity development" (Knudson & Terrell, 2012).

This creates a real issue because when a disturbance in identity development happens, we lose who we are. We can become a chameleon to be all things to all people but never true to ourselves. To fit in at work, we overachieve to show our boss our value. At a family event, we become the neutral party, the peacemaker. When we are out with friends, they get the fun, outgoing, life-of-the-party side of us. Constantly changing who we are according to our environment only leaves us feeling lost and dead inside.

Our poacher (Satan) is calculated and sly. He masks codependency as things we value: helping family, friends, protector, provider...the list is endless. He watches and waits for us to walk through the well-decorated trap, feeding our insecurities. All too often, we do. In an effort to help others, we begin to lose ourselves, and what started as good intentions becomes an idol propelling our purpose.

Satan set the snare, and we walked right through it. Pleasing man has become our idol, and the infection of chasing man for value, love, or acceptance poisons our hearts and clouds our judgment. The harder we try to prove our worth, the more worthless and unappreciated we feel.

It pulls us further from God and keeps us wounded and in a toxic cycle of seeking healing from man instead of God.

Proverbs 29:25 (NIV) says, "Fear of man will prove to be a snare, but whoever trusts in the Lord is kept safe." That is such a powerful statement. That sentence alone tells us how deadly seeking man's approval is. Our identity can't be connected to a title because then we choose to make man our God instead of trusting God.

Pleasing man is a never-ending battle. The more we give of ourselves, the more they take. The more we compromise or conform, the more they demand. Eventually, we are left looking in the mirror at a stranger with lost dreams, hopes, and loneliness as we try to be the "happiness" in someone else's life.

That evening the boy put me in a headlock, I learned two things. One, boys don't stay little forever. They grow up and become much stronger than women by nature (God designed them to protect us). Two, pride is toxic, and codependency gives us a false sense of self. For weeks and months, I refused to hang out with my friends, using chores or homework as an excuse to hide my wounded ego. I played my failure over and over. How would I protect my siblings? Or myself? I had attached my value and self-worth to my family as "the protector." Without that, I was nothing.

That snare choked me slowly my entire life as I painfully fought to gain validation for my performance.

Eventually, I understood that my validation, my dependency, needed to be rooted in God and Him alone. I had to trust His way for me even when I didn't understand it. Then, I experienced the deep healing in my heart and freedom from the snare laid before me.

Reflection: Are you struggling to prove your worth? Are you saying yes to demands placed on you at the cost of your needs or happiness? Have you asked yourself why you chose to sacrifice your well-being, mental health, and peace for the convenience of others? Reread Proverbs 29:25. Ask God to reveal the snare in your life. Then, wash it under the blood and release it to God.

Prayer: Father God, forgive me for the idols I have placed before you. Please remove the snare of _____ (fill in the blank as God revealed to you). Please deliver me from the need to seek the approval and validation of man over you. Help me find your face in all circumstances set before me so that I won't fall back into the trap set before me.

Today, I choose to chase the truth and keep my eyes on you. I ask that you still my heart and fill it with your peace and power. Allow me to feel your presence when I am feeling alone. Give me a word to remind me of your goodness and love in my times of trouble. Lord, give me the power to stand against the temptations and toxic people in my life.

In Jesus' name, I pray. Amen.

Attitude Adjustment

"The problem is not the problem; The problem
is your attitude about the problem."
– Johnny Depp (Jack Sparrow), *Pirates of the Caribbean*

"It's easy to learn to protect yourself and fight, but it's harder to deal with pain or disappointment caused by others. How we handle these disappointments matters," my children's sensei once said. In other words, we need to train our mind as much as our body. What good is being a black belt, strong in stature, if we're fragile in mind and character?

For the last two years, I have watched my children diligently train in a martial art form called Kempo. This type believes that our mental toughness and character are just as important (if not more important) than our physical ability to fight. Following each class, there is a breakout session in which the sensei discusses a multitude of challenges the students will face outside the studio. He presents a conflict and has the students come up with a solution. They must listen and talk out their choices. These sessions build character and communication skills while talking about hard topics. For this reason, I choose to keep my kids in his program as opposed to others.

Let's get real for a minute. All of us have felt the sting of betrayal, the pain of failed expectations, and the disappointment of not being enough. From a young age, we have "worked for the approval of another." Let's play a snapshot of life from toddlerhood to young adulthood. A toddler colors a picture and runs to Mommy, excited to give her their latest masterpiece. Then, they eagerly await a response: "Wow, sweetie, this is beautiful. Good job."

The elementary school child brings home writing or even has

you sit with them to practice reading, awaiting your feedback, your praise, and wondering, *Am I doing it right? Was that good?*

The middle schooler and high schooler wonder, *Am I missing the mark?* As they become more independent and blaze their own path in this world, they seek approval from peers, teammates, teachers, and sometimes parents. But the voices that are most important to them mold the decisions they make.

Finally, they become adults and often operate in that same mindset. Our worth is given by man, by the peer group we are trying to impress.

Will my boss find me worthy of a promotion? Am I a good parent, or have I messed up my child? Am I a good lover, or could my spouse have done better? Am I attractive enough, or do I need to lose weight?

We consistently seek others' approval to ensure that we are heard, valued, respected, and loved. There is nothing wrong with any of those things. The problem comes when those desires are met with resistance, broken promises, or failed expectations.

How do we handle a promotion that passed us over when we feel we were the most qualified? Or disappointment of always being the one people count on when things go wrong, but when we are broken and need encouragement, not one person stands by our side?

I can almost guarantee it produces anger, frustration, and disappointment. The trust we have in people has been fractured, and each failed expectation creates another fracture until we isolate ourselves to protect what's left of our broken hearts.

The problem we face is often just a piece of a bigger picture. How we view the offense determines our course of action.

Are we viewing the problem through the broken lenses of insecurities and hurt pride, or are we looking through the lens of humility, choosing to leave it at Jesus's feet and trust that he will make sense of the situation and that the outcome will be in your favor for his glory?

This is a daily exercise for me. I am the person who sees a

problem at work, church, or even with friends, and will offer a solution or myself to help. I have done whatever it takes to prove I am the best at whatever I put my hands on so that people knew I was dependable and could get the job done. This was especially true in ministry. I wanted so badly to serve God, to have a purpose, that I quickly overextended myself in multiple ministries so that the church's needs were met. I made "friends" in leadership who would always tap on my shoulder when balls were dropped, knowing I was dependable. I always showed up ready to help wherever.

So, imagine my surprise when those same friends were too busy when I needed them the most. Caring for my father in my home on hospice was one of the hardest things I walked through. I felt like my life was unraveling and I had no control. I needed friends, help, meals…anything, and they were all too busy with ministry and life. I walked that road feeling alone and hurt.

I realized that always pleasing others came at a great price. Someone always needed something. A ball was always dropped, and I never had peace. Always being the one to show up without reciprocation left me consistently offended, let down, and bitter.

That's when I realized I held others to the same work ethic I had for myself, and if they did not measure up, I would internally accuse them of being lazy or uncommitted. In reality, they may have just had healthy boundaries.

When I was in pain and mourning, I received very little support or encouragement. I grew resentful and distant. With every disappointment, I pulled further away, cutting off the people who hurt me until I could count the number of people I spoke with on one hand. "I refuse to be used, a sucker, taken for granted. They say they love me but can't be bothered to call or help me in my darkest moments. Who needs friends like that? I am better off without them."

Comments like that would play on repeat in my mind, keeping

me resentful of the people in my life who failed me without even knowing.

I was hurt. I told myself lies and believed them. I carried pride and entitlement without even realizing it. Who am I to hold someone to a standard I made? The only standard we should live for is set by God. Yet I was guilty of the very thing others had done to cause me pain.

When we are raised in "an eye for an eye and tooth for a tooth" culture, we can forget it's not our place to be judge, jury, and executioner. We need to consistently seek God in all places so that we may model Him, especially in times of disappointment and discontentment.

Paul speaks of living a new life in Ephesians, chapter four. He begins by saying not to live like the gentiles in futility in their thinking because it is darkened in understanding. Then, he explains that this leads to a separation from God because of their ignorance and the hardening of their hearts. This way of life led the gentiles to rely on their own ways, giving way to whatever pleasure they desired. When we harden our hearts and God is far away from us, we are no longer sensitive to his Spirit and, therefore, seek out things to gratify our flesh in the moment. Maybe it is a drink, a smoke, or even a loose tongue and cursing another out. Whatever you rely on to fix the pain, it takes the Lord's place.

Paul reminds us, "That, however, is not the way of life you learned when you heard about Christ and were taught in him in accordance with the truth that is in Jesus. You were taught, with regard to your former way of life, to put off your old self, which is being corrupted by its deceitful desires; to be made new in the attitude of your minds; and to put on the new self, created to be like God in true righteousness and holiness" (Ephesians 4:20-24 NIV).

Putting off our old self does not mean we won't feel pain and disappointment. It means we will no longer be controlled by deceptive desires that once held us in bondage, that we will trust in

God to lead our lives and follow in his footsteps. It means that even in the ugly moments, we will run to the Lord instead of the bottle or running our mouths.

Being made new in our minds means that we will operate under a new standard—one that God has set for us, extending grace instead of wrath, understanding instead of resentment—and learn to guard our hearts by asking the Lord to give us wisdom in all things as we continue to grow to be more like Him.

Reflection: Have you been stewing on an offense you have no control over? Have you resorted to old patterns of thinking and methods of making things right? Have they worked out in your favor or left you feeling even more alone, angry, and resentful? If you're stuck in the pain of failed expectation or betrayal, reread Ephesians, chapter 4. Know that you are a new creation and there is a standard you should be walking in.

Prayer: Lord, it is so easy to get angry when things don't work out as planned, when people let us down or hurt us, when people lie to us and manipulate us. Forgive me for my unforgiveness and resentment. I forgive (all the names of the people who hurt you) for (how they hurt you). It is so easy to fall back into old patterns of self-preservation and protection.

Help me to move past the pain so I don't make the same mistakes twice. Today, I surrender the need to have control of my life. I surrender to your will for my life and ask you to teach me how to handle conflict with grace and understanding. Please give me wisdom in every circumstance and peace to navigate the storms before me. Help me to love, trust, see, and forgive like you.

Please heal the fractured parts of my heart so I can grow deeper in my relationships with others.

In Jesus' name, Amen.

Get in the Cage

"No point punching things you can't see."
– James J. Braddock, *Cinderella Man*

I should have been anxious, frustrated, or even hopeful. Instead, I felt nothing, completely indifferent, numb. I responded to the techs and doctors almost robotically while my mind wondered, *What else will they find wrong with me? Will I live to see my children grow and get married?*

This last year, I was diagnosed with lupus, Sjogren's, and Reynaud's. I went from crushing my CrossFit goals to not being able to lift, jump, or run without losing feeling in my arms and legs. No matter how my coaches modified the workout, I could never complete it. My frustration soared to an all-time high as I lost control of my body and began fighting an unseen opponent.

I refused to give up—I am a fighter. Every day, I pushed through, and every night, I did the same at the gym. Until it finally happened. While jumping rope, I lost feeling in my legs and fell, injuring my knee and ankle and preventing me from working out at all. The doctors sent me to see yet another specialist, who ordered an EMG (Electromyography test). This test measured the electrical activity of my muscles and nerves and would hopefully tell us why I lost feeling doing sports activities.

I was tired. Tired of losing control of my body, tired of not being able to keep up the pace, of hurting, getting hurt, and the uncertainty of it all.

I was losing my hair, fighting abnormal swelling, an ungodly amount of joint pain, and constant exhaustion. My body rapidly felt weaker with no explanation. Every day was a fight to get up— fighting pain, fear, and disappointment. Every day, I looked at my husband and children and fought to get through it so I did not fail them. Every night, I cried myself to sleep, wondering if this disease would claim my life as it had my aunt's.

The depression crept in quietly, suddenly, and without warning, took root.

By day, I would claim God had me in his hands, and I would overcome this. It would not be my portion, my end. By night, I would wonder if God heard my prayers or if I meant anything to Him at all. Defeated, I crawled into bed each night, ready to be far away from everyone…including my family.

I lay there like a wounded soldier waiting for this test to end, wondering what the outcome would be. Each negative diagnosis I received stirred my faith, and when I did not receive immediate healing, I indirectly questioned God's love for me. I knew He was there. I knew He could heal me if He chose, but maybe, just maybe, I was not worth His touch.

This is exactly where the enemy wants us—in a place of defeat, alone, and in doubt, so he can keep our eyes off the creator and on our circumstances.

The technician cheerfully interrupted my thoughts. "Do you do CrossFit?" She pointed at my hat with the name of my CrossFit box on it.

I looked at her smiling face. "Yeah, I did. I love it and want to get back to it without losing feeling in my body."

She nodded. "I can't imagine how this must feel. I kickbox. I train at a gym called Nine Rounds. I go after work. It's my therapy. If I couldn't train, I would be miserable too."

"Really? Kickboxing? That's awesome. It must be hard but so much fun."

"Well, I'm sure no harder than CrossFit. You guys are a different breed." We both laughed. "I am a fighter; I like to fight. I may not always win. But training equips me to improve. It makes me stronger and forces me to persevere. CrossFit strikes me as similar. We don't give up. We push past the discomfort and overcome one obstacle at a time."

I was speechless, overwhelmed with peace I had not felt in a long time. Then, the Lord whispered, "Nine rounds...the fight is not yours, it's mine. This will be what you write."

Things turned for me that day. God used that woman to open my eyes and help me see I was wasting my energy fighting a moving, invisible opponent when the fight was not mine to start with.

Matthew 26:52 (CSB) says, "Then Jesus told him, "Put your sword back in its place because all who take up the sword will perish by the sword." I am not fighting with a literal weapon, yet I dare say the outcome can be the same. A sword is a deadly weapon in the hands of someone trained or angry enough to use it as such. Our words hold that same power in our lives. What we tell ourselves and speak over our lives can kill our Spirit and defeat us or bring us peace. Whenever something robs our peace, we must ask ourselves, is this our fight? Or are we wasting our energy on an unseen opponent?

It's OK to be afraid of the unknown. We can still overcome if we choose to trust the Lord.

> "When I am afraid,
> I will trust in you.
> In God, whose word I praise,
> in God I trust; I will not be afraid.
> What can mere mortals do to me?"
> (Psalm 56:3-4 CSB)

I will never forget that moment in the hospital room, the day the Lord visited me through a technician and reminded me of His love and strength. The day my eyes opened to see I was loved even if I didn't understand what was happening to me. That day, I chose to put my trust back in God. I wish I could say it has been all roses and sunshine since, but it hasn't. I have continued down a road of unexplained and complicated diagnoses. However, every time I am afraid, uncertain, or struggling with depression or anger, I surrender to God and choose to trust Him. I believe His way is best. The journey may not always be easy, but I know this to be true. We are not alone, and we will overcome.

Reflection: Are you fighting an unseen opponent? Are you swinging a sword of doubt, fear, anxiety, depression, or resentment? Are you doubting the love or presence of God in your life?

Fear and faith ask the same thing of us. How will we respond to the unknown? The choice is ours.

Reread Psalm 56:3-4, reflect on David's words, and lead by his example. Choose to trust in God amid uncertainty and fear.

Prayer: Father, I ask you to meet me wherever I sit. Permeate the space I am in and fill it with your peace and presence. The battles I face belong to you, yet it is so hard to not pick up the sword and start swinging. Help me find peace and comfort during my trials. Help me see your hand and face in unexpected places like the doctor's office, a street sign, or even a coworker. Lord, as I lean in and choose to trust you, strengthen me in Spirit and mind.

Lord, I love you. Help me walk in a way that pleases you. Help me walk in faith.

In Jesus' name, Amen.

Lock In

"You always have a plan in your mind and you never know how your opponent is going to respond, but one thing I can tell you is I'm going to finish the fight."
– Alexa Grasso

Alexa Grasso was the first Mexican women's lightweight UFC champion. She made an impact on young women in Mexico and around the world—a female in a male-dominated sport, never giving up and chasing her dreams. This is what made me love her. She was inspirational, humble, and strong.

In a culture where women are not known for fighting professionally, she showed it was possible with hard work and commitment. It was a classic underdog story, and who doesn't love one of those?

On September seventeenth, I watched the rematch between her and the former champion, Valentina Shevchenko. Shevchenko (known to be the most dominating fighter in their weight class) wanted her title and belt back, but Grasso planned to keep it!

Shevchenko was a force to be reckoned with, and I would dare say Grasso's Goliath. She was ready to reclaim her belt, and it showed. Grasso didn't let Shevchenko shake her (or at least didn't show it).

Blood splattered across the mat as Grasso took a blow to the face. With each strike Shevchenko made, Grasso relentlessly found her way to her feet and continued fighting back. Blood spatter on their clothing revealed the power behind their punches and their intensity and passion for their sport. The entire fight was nail-biting. At times, I had to close my eyes, but each fighter left everything they had on the mat. Neither of them took their eye off the other. The fight concluded in a rare draw. After the back-and-forth battle, the last round gave Grasso the winning advantage, tying the scorecards allowing Grasso to keep the belt. The arena went wild, and I jumped in excitement that Grasso once again walked away with the belt., 47

I can't imagine the hours of training, the tough choices, and the sacrifices she made to prepare for this fight. She didn't know what her opponent had in store for her in the rematch, but her focus remained on how she could improve what was already in her rather than what was against her. She trusted her coaches while they prepared her for the big day. If she had not listened to her coaches and put in the work, the fight could have ended differently. Her victory came from commitment and obedience.

We all face opponents daily. Life stresses, jobs, children, relationship troubles. Some of us feel we defeated our opponent—trauma, depression, anxiety, unresolved anger, and even fractured trust—yet they come back unannounced, ready for a rematch. But our victory swings on the hinges of our commitment and obedience.

Just like preparing for a physical fight requires physical and self-discipline to win, so does our spiritual walk. In Proverbs 4:25-27 (NIV), Solomon instructs Rehoboam to stay focused ("locked in") on what's before him.

> *"Let your eyes look straight ahead;*
> *fix your gaze directly before you.*
> *Give careful thought to the paths for your feet*
> *and be steadfast in all your ways.*
> *Do not turn to the right or the left;*
> *keep your foot from evil."*

We are given simple directions: We must keep our eyes in front of us (on God) and not the circumstances around us. Other broken people can't help us heal from past pain or trauma; other insecure people can't affirm who we are. Our eyes should be locked in on Him. We must be careful where we place our feet. The places we go and the people we surround ourselves with matter. If we tread on the grounds of toxic places (bars, parties, clubs), we can expect to be led down a destructive path of impure, toxic, or evil patterns of living. Just like Grasso was locked in at the Noche UFC event against her opponent, we need to be locked into what God has for us. Even if we can't see it. Even if we don't know what to expect. We must be willing to trust our Father and the coaches He places in our lives (mentors, pastors, trusted leaders) to guide us through when things are tough.

As Solomon says, do not turn right or left. Let's commit to keeping our eyes on God, trust our coach, and know that His ways are better than ours. Now, LOCK IN!

Reflection: You may not always start a fight, but you can finish it. Take a few minutes to reflect on circumstances that present themselves against you. Has this opponent been a repeat offender? Has it robbed you of peace and joy or made you critical? How can Proverbs 4:25-27 change that fight? Where is your coach in this fight? Have you forgotten to keep your eyes on His directions? If so, are you willing to commit your way back to God and allow Him to finish this fight for you?

Prayer: Heavenly Father, forgive me for taking my eyes off you. Forgive me for losing sight of the vision or promise you gave me. Please set that vision on fire in my soul. Please ignite me with your Spirit so I may hear your voice thunder within me. I pray that you keep my feet from treading on evil and my eyes on the things you desire for me so I do not get lost in the distractions before me. Remind me of my purpose and your plan for me. Please give me the strength to face my opponent and the confidence to know you will defeat them through me.

Fill me with your perfect peace.

In Jesus' name, I pray. Amen.

ROUND 9

Champion

Inside Out

"A healthy outside starts from the inside."
– Robert Urich

I saw an interview once where a young man stopped fit people on the beach and asked, "What did you do to obtain a body like that?"

Lots of people gave quick answers, but an older gentleman said, "I don't overeat or eat sweets. I stay away from processed foods, alcohol, and sugary drinks. I don't compromise sleep or make excuses. I eat whole, nutrient-dense, fresh foods, food prep, and commit to working out two hours a day, five days a week. I chose to make my health a priority."

He had me clapping in my living room. (If I had been there, he would have gotten a big high five.) This gentleman wanted the world to know it wasn't about how hard he worked out in the gym; rather, it was what he didn't do. If more people understood that about sacrifice as much as work, more people would have the results they want. Our health, physically, mentally, and spiritually, is a discipline. The same discipline athletes have in training seasons.

Fighters train to get into the octagon, mat, or ring. Athletes train to perform on fields, courts, or in water. All training requires an ungodly amount of dedication and discipline. Nothing happens by accident. They put in the work, and lots of it. And what they put in their bodies affects how they perform. How much rest they get impacts their recovery, and their commitment and discipline determine their success. Putting the work in shows in the results.

So why do we think differently about our spiritual or mental state? Ephesians 5:29 (NIV) says, "After all, no one ever hated their own body, but they feed and care for their body, just as Christ does the church."

If we struggle with depression, anxiety, or anger, the last thing we should be listening to is music focused on anger, sadness, or unfaithfulness. We should stay away from shows or social media posts that fill our minds with fear or insecurities. We definitely should not be isolating and self-medicating with comfort foods, drinks, or other substances.

This is our life, our journey, and whether we believe it or not, we are in control. We need to channel our inner athlete. Quitting is not an option. Staying stuck is not an option. Our goal, why we fight, is to have a whole, full, and prosperous life.

Training season has started, and it begins by healing and strengthening our injured hearts. It's time to commit to our healing and get stronger again. No excuses.

First, we must feed ourselves well, just like an athlete. Stay away from junk, i.e., social media, and feed yourself the Word daily. Keep a journal for thoughts and prayers. Continue speaking to God. Even though you may feel He is not listening, He is. If you can't read (you don't have the headspace), listen to the Word or sermons on podcast. Just get the Word in your heart. What goes in comes out. If we keep feeding our minds toxic things, we will stay in that mindset.

Next, we need to connect to our church. Don't forsake the assembly of the saints. Get plugged in. Be a part of a small group, join a serve team, and connect with other believers. No one is alone. These people can pray with you, encourage you, and walk with you. Speak with a pastor. Allow your shepherd to guide you. God placed him as a shepherd for a reason. Follow him as he follows God.

Counseling is one more training tool under the belt. Filter what advice they give and hold it to the Word of God. Speak about it with trusted friends who can assist with accountability in this walk.

Getting through this time can be hard, but church family and professionals can guide us and help us up and out.

God is for us, not against us. We can and will overcome. Don't give up—keep moving forward one step at a time.

Reflection: Ephesians 5:29 mentions feeding and caring for your body. Get a pen and write down the following:

- What are some of the toxic things you feed yourself? (list 5)
- What are some lies you are choosing to believe or things spoken over you that caused pain?
- What things are you telling yourself that keep you from moving forward?
- How has this affected your mental, spiritual, and physical health?

Once you have finished, remember that Hebrews 4:13 (NIV) says, "Nothing in all creation is hidden from God's sight. Everything is uncovered and laid bare before the eyes of him to whom we must give account."

God sees you. He sees your shortcomings, failures, and heart, yet He still loves you. He still desires a relationship with you and wants you to be whole and happy. "We love because he first loved us" (1 John 4:19 NIV). Man's love is conditional, but God's is unconditional. Allow Him in to restore your broken heart.

Prayer: Father in heaven, please forgive me my shortcomings, the ones I am aware of and the ones I am not. Help me enter your presence. Please rest upon me and begin to restore the peace and joy I once had. I ask that you show me how to love myself and renounce the lies I have been deceived into believing. Speak to me so that I may no longer feel alone but know you are standing alongside me. Shatter the chains that keep me bound and restore the hope I found in you.

In Jesus' name, I pray. Amen.

Combat Indifference

*"Life has many ways of testing a person's will, either by having
nothing happen at all or by having everything happen all at once."*
— Paulo Coelho, *The Winner Stands Alone*

R egardless of what preachers say, we don't always go from
mountaintop to mountaintop. Some seasons feel more like
we are drowning in the ocean or lost in our valley. It's hardship
after hardship, bad report after bad report, and heartbreak after
heartbreak, wondering if we will ever catch a break. We grow
mentally, physically, and spiritually exhausted. Blinded to truth and
hope, we begin hardening our hearts and risk becoming completely
indifferent.

> *"For this people's heart has become calloused;*
> *they hardly hear with their ears,*
> *and they have closed their eyes.*
> *Otherwise they might see with their eyes,*
> *hear with their ears,*
> *understand with their hearts*
> *and turn, and I would heal them."*
> *(Matthew 13:15 NIV)*

I wish I had Matthew 13:15 when I was in my long valley season,
when I ran on empty and continued giving of myself to prove my
worth. I gave more than I had in ministry, trying to show our pastor
I was dependable, reliable, and a great leader. At work, I would pick up
dropped balls to prove I could handle the workload and stress. When
I got home, my family got what was left of me as I halfheartedly tried
to meet my husband's needs and dutifully took care of my kids.

Feeling inadequate, overworked, and underappreciated, I slowly became indifferent, robotically waking up to tend to my family, going through the motions at work, and then serving in ministry. My life was full yet empty. Ministry felt more like politics rather than serving God. "God does not call the qualified; He qualifies the called," I heard from the pulpit, yet I watched as members slowly grew cold and lost passion for serving because they were discouraged from pursuing their passion and gift and filtered into an area where the church needed other skill sets they possed (like admin skills), skills they had yet brought them no life. I remember preaching at women's events and district events while in school, but when the district had a leadership conference, I was unable to attend because I did not hold the title of pastor on paper. Our pastor's wife fought for me to be there, but they would not budge.

It made me think, IF God qualifies us, not just credentials, then who is man to disqualify us or discourage us from pursuing the purpose God placed in us? Could the church really be more shallow than the unsaved? My soul ran dry. I had nothing left to give, and nothing mattered. Everything I did became a task on my to-do list that needed to be crossed off before I could check out for the night, repeated again the next day. I was not living, simply existing. I could not see the truth in my pastors' words, my husband's love, or even my children's adoration. In order to reevaluate my life, I stepped down from ministry and left my job.

I had allowed the troubles of life and conflicts at work to callous my heart. Withdrawing from friends and family, I continued doing what was expected of me while dying inside.

In desperation, I cried out, "God, if you are even real, make me feel something, anything. Why do I even exist?" That night, I dreamed, and the Lord revealed to me I was on this earth for Him, to serve Him, to teach others who He is and His goodness. To snatch people from the darkness. I would spread the Gospel, preach, and teach. But it had to start in my home with my children (as they had begun to resent God and ministry)

When I woke up, I was no longer indifferent but angry! At least I could feel again. How was I to do all this if I just stepped down from leadership? In that season, I had a choice. I could stay how I was, frustrated, unhappy, angry at the world, or change the direction of my life, submitting to God and fully trusting Him. The choice was mine. Only I had the power to get out of this valley, and the same is true for us all.

We can't control the circumstances in our lives, but we can control where we place our trust. We have a choice: we either trust in God and believe in His character (even when things don't make sense and we don't understand) or we don't.

If we believe that God is a loving, just, and faithful God, then we must also believe He will heal our hearts, right the wrongs, and make us whole again. Is it not better than living in sorrow, anger, indifference, or pain? Is it not better to take the chance of walking out our faith, especially in our darkness, believing in the character of God? So, open your eyes and look around at all God created (even if you're mad at Him). Speak to Him (even through the tears) and listen for His voice. Submit your heart to Him and release the situation so He can heal you.

Reflection: Does it feel like nothing matters? Have you become indifferent, going through the motions in life.? It won't get better until you see God's Word as truth, until you open your eyes and surrender your heart to the Lord. If you can't see past your situation, speak to a counselor. Allow them to shed light on what may be holding you in this jail cell. Reflect on Romans 12:12. "Rejoice in hope, be patient in tribulation, be constant in prayer" (Romans 12:12 NIV).

Find an elder you trust to speak into your life. Allow that person to pray for you and with you. Champions have teams, so find your team and win this match.

Prayer: Heavenly Father, I am so far from perfect. I need your grace and mercy every day. I need fresh revelation from you every day. I pray today that you open the eyes of your readers so they can see you even in the trials they face. I pray that you speak loudly to them and bring their heart's understanding as it says in Matthew 13:15. Please heal their hearts and restore their joy.

In Jesus' name, I pray. Amen.

Vantage Point

"Getting knocked down in life is a given. Getting up and moving forward is a choice."
— Zig Ziglar, *Born to Win*

Every time the boys and I watch a fight, we get frustrated with the fighters who get knocked down and beat on with no clear plan to get into the fight. They become their opponent's punching bag. It doesn't have to be that way. Every fighter has a team that trained them for months, years, to be where they are. The team got them that far and helped them master their skill. They walked them down the aisle and stood in their corner. They have a vantage point the fighter doesn't see while face-to-face with their opponent. They see weaknesses and patterns the fighter misses.

If a fighter wants to maximize their success, they must fully trust their coaches and listen to them on and off the mat.

So why are we surprised when life's trials and challenges knock us down? Why are we surprised when we struggle with depression, anxiety, grief, anger, or anything else? Unfortunately, many churches have created a culture where Christians (if they have enough faith) can live from glory to glory and mountaintop to mountaintop. They have set the illusion that, once we get saved, the sanctification process is done overnight and we are freed from struggles and strong holds. We somehow expect to be superhuman and perfect, fully sanctified, yet show no grace for the broken.

Scripture says, "Beloved, do not be surprised at the fiery trial when it comes upon you to test you, as though something strange were happening to you" (1 Peter 4:12 ESV). In other words, surprise blows will hit us in life. We will struggle with ugly things that some churches don't care to talk about. Our own Christian friends or "church people" will knock us down.

The good news is that our coach has the vantage point. He stands in our corner, and every time the opponent of life knocks us down, He waits for us to come to Him. God is rooting for us. He wants us to live a life of victory, not defeat.

So, if life constantly beats us down, maybe it's because we are not listening to the one who has the vantage point. Maybe our trust is in our own ability and not in the Lord.

Reflection: Take a moment to write down the areas tripping you up, the battles that repeat in your life.

Scripture is full of stories of God giving victory to His people: David and Goliath, Moses splitting the Red Sea, Noah, Jericho, and more. Gideon defeating the Midianite army is one of my favorites.

"The LORD spoke to Gideon. He said, 'With the help of the 300 men who lapped up the water I will save you. I will hand the Midianites over to you. Let all the other men go home.' So Gideon sent those Israelites home. But he kept the 300 men. They took over the supplies and trumpets the others had left" (Judges 7:7 NIRV).

Reflect on this scripture. The Lord spoke to Gideon. He still speaks to us. Are we listening? What is the Lord promising you about your battle? The Lord gave directions, and though the odds were stacked against Gideon and could have cost him his life, he followed the Lord's orders, leading to victory. What directions have the Lord revealed to you? Are you ready to follow?

Prayer: Father in heaven, I thank you for being patient with me. For your continued grace and love during all the times I chose not to listen or got distracted by my own plans. Please forgive me for not being sensitive to your Word and not listening to your direction. The fight lying before me is not mine but yours. Please show me how to overcome so I no longer feel the pain and pressure of this fight. Please give me the victory so I am no longer in silent pain. Thank you in advance for the victory I will see as I walk in obedience to you.

In Jesus' name, I pray. Amen.

ROUND 9: FIGHT

"Champions aren't made in the gyms. Champions are made from something they have deep inside them—a desire, a dream, a vision."
— Muhammad Ali (World Heavyweight Champion Boxer)

Fighters fight to win. They spend countless days and hours putting their bodies under intense stress training in preparation for the fight. All while going through the same pains we face—loss, betrayal, depression, anxiety, indifference, and more.

Yet despite all the storms life hands them, they have a choice: fight or fold. Driven by passion, they fight. Fight to win, fight to earn a title, and fight to keep it.

Bertolt Brecht said, "He who fights, can lose. He who doesn't fight, has already lost." That quote reignites me because it can apply to our lives in many ways. A fighter chances loss when stepping in the ring, but if they only dream of becoming a champion and never take the steps to do it, they stay a dreamer, not a fighter.

We are no different. All too often, we forget that Jesus died a brutal death and rose again so we may be reconciled to God. He is our champion. His death was not a fable or story of hope. It was the story of how to live. Christ's death and our salvation are access to the throne room. We have been granted the gift of the Holy Spirit and, therefore, have a champion inside us.

We face real fears and battle real monsters. They just happen to be inside us. But we have a real God who fights for us, equips us, and guides us every step of the way if we listen and allow Him to.

David earned victory with a sling and a stone, Gideon with three hundred men against thousands. Moses parted the sea. The walls of Jericho were brought down by a shout. God fed the multitudes.

Shadrach, Meshach, and Abednego were saved from the fiery furnace because GOD WAS WITH THEM.

And He is still with us today.

Ephesians 6:10-12 (NLT) tells us: "A final word: Be strong in the Lord and in his mighty power. Put on all of God's armor so that you will be able to stand firm against all strategies of the devil. For we are not fighting against flesh-and-blood enemies, but against evil rulers and authorities of the unseen world, against mighty powers in this dark world, and against evil spirits in the heavenly places."

We can't expect to defeat a challenger without taking direction from our Father. The Bible tells us to put on the full armor of God so we can stand firm against the devil's strategies. That means all things coming against us to take us down. If we do not protect ourselves, how do we expect to stand? If a fighter is told to wear a mouthguard but chooses to fight without it, whose fault is it when their teeth get knocked out of their face? We fight against real darkness, real evil, and we need to know how to stand.

Ephesians 6:13 (NLT) says, "Therefore, put on every piece of God's armor so you will be able to resist the enemy in the time of evil. Then, after the battle you will still be standing firm." The power already resides in us. The tools were provided, but we must choose to use them. Every battle won in scripture resulted from obedience to the Lord. Directions were given; they trusted and obeyed and, therefore, obtained victory. When they did not, they found trouble.

Bottom line, we won't always feel like the Lord is with us. We won't always feel like praying or praising. We definitely won't always feel like reading. But not one champion would say they looked forward to training while injured or that training through a divorce, death, or addiction was easy.

No, a champion grinds even when they don't want to. They work through the pain and overcome the obstacles standing in the way. Their team carries them through every day and holds them accountable.

We have a team too. God leads us in battle, is the source of our power, and gives us the authority. Trusted mentors and pastors keep us accountable, acting as our coaches and growing us where we are weak. Trusted friends can sharpen us, pray with us, and help us in our walk with the Lord. And if needed, professional counselors are wonderful at helping us identify issues we missed and providing tools to help us overcome (just make sure it lines up with the Word of God).

Now that we've forged a winning team, the power lies within us. Champion, it's time to suit up and claim victory!

Reflection: Are you struggling to feel like a champion? Do you feel alone? Have you isolated and aren't sure who to trust? Read Ephesians 10:18. What part of the armor are you missing? Why? Write down how you can change that, and then begin to pray.

Prayer: Heavenly Father, trust does not come easy for me. Past pains and betrayals have left me broken and keep me bound. Please heal those places in my heart. I ask that you provide clarity about who can guide me in troubling times. Bring to memory a pastor, leader, or confidant that will come alongside me and strengthen me in you.

I ask that you speak to me and remind me of who I am in you. Reveal yourself in a way that only you can. Move mountains that are immovable, open closed doors, create paths in the wilderness, and restore all that was stolen from me. Please strengthen me and grow my faith. Give me the victory I need in my life.

In Jesus' name, I pray. Amen.

Champion,

Thank you for choosing to take the journey of healing with me. Remember, we won't always see a fight (life storm) as a win. We won't always understand why things unfold as they do. But when the weight is too much for us to bear, we don't have to do it alone. We have the team God equipped us with. Continue trusting in the Lord regardless of what you see in the natural.

Keep moving forward one step at a time. Believe that everything stolen from you will be restored, rebuilt, and victorious. "The Lord appeared to us in the past, saying: 'I have loved you with an everlasting love; I have drawn you with unfailing kindness. I will build you up again'" (Jeremiah 31:3-4 NIV).

Julie Whitley

About the Author

Julie Whitley is a wife, mother, coach, and trainer. She was raised in a home where her family supported and helped people who struggled with various forms of mental illness. Julie not only walked through the dark times of anxiety and deep depression, but she has also spent years mentoring those stuck in those places. Julie wants the world to know Christians are not exempt from dark thoughts or crippling anxiety. A real fight is happening in our minds, and Julie wants her readers to know Christians are not exempt from experiencing these trials. But we do have the vantage point. The fight is His, not ours.

Julie has completed two years of ministry development, interned under Reverend Joel Johnson, and led Connect Groups and Women's Ministry at her home church. In addition, Julie has hosted and spoken at women's workshops and district conventions. In her free time, she feeds her competitive nature by pushing her body to new limits at CrossFit and spending quality time with her boys and husband.

Printed in the United States
by Baker & Taylor Publisher Services